THE FAMILY MINISTRY PLAYBOOK

FOR PARTNERING WITH PARENTS

BY PHIL BELL

randall house

114 Bush Rd | Nashville, TN 37217
randallhouse.com

Printed in the United States of America

Unless otherwise noted, all Scripture quotations are taken from the Holy Bible, New
Living Translation (NLT), copyright ©1996, 2004, 2007, 2013, 2015 by Tyndale
House Foundation. Used by permission of Tyndale House Publishers, Inc., Carol
Stream, Illinois 60188. All rights reserved.

ISBN 13: 9781614841173

TABLE OF CONTENTS

FOREWORD

I'm old enough to have seen an incredible maturing in youth ministry. I became a Christian and started in youth work during the "Jesus Movement"—a movement that changed the way churches did outreach and missions as well as youth and children's ministry. Today youth and children's ministry is a staple of every healthy, growing church. But long before even I was around, the pioneers of youth work led the way in warning the church to reach out to kids or risk losing them. Their message was prophetic.

When I came onto the youth ministry scene, books about youth ministry were just beginning to have a more practical focus. Many of us were still making things up as we went, but we were beginning to write down for others what we were doing. Some of the best youth ministry leadership was coming from outside the church through parachurch organizations, but people were rapidly taking that leadership into the church. Today, however, the youth and children's movement gets its leadership from within churches all over the world. And some of the strongest leadership voices are coming from outside the United States.

Now we're witnessing a brand-new movement of God called family ministry. Over a decade ago voices in leadership started talking about the need to partner with parents in youth and children's ministry. We knew the need was important, but very few had any idea how to do it. Plus, the first books written on the subject were weak on offering practical advice, focusing more on declaring the need—just as the pioneers of youth work did in the early days of youth ministry.

The Family Ministry Playbook is a much-needed book written by someone who works in the church to make family ministry a reality every day. I remember well the first time I met my friend Phil Bell. What a voice! Even though he now lives in the United States, Phil has an incredible British accent. His voice is kind, positive, authentic, and caring, just as this book is. It's a practical book where you can find help on each page for implementing an effective family ministry in your church. Its message comes from the voice of a leader. Also, those who read it will find it to be incredibly helpful.

At HomeWord we have two sayings that get me going each day: "One of the major purposes of the church is to mentor parents; the parents mentor their children while partnering with the church, and the legacy of faith continues from generation to generation," and "When you reach the family, you reach the world." The family ministry movement is growing and changing even faster than youth and children's ministry did in its early days, with some family ministry conferences having larger attendance than conferences for youth and children's ministry. I'm thrilled for the new voices of leadership—such as Phil's—that are speaking into this ministry movement today.

Jim Burns, Ph.D.
President, HomeWord
Dana Point, California

Author's Note

A COUPLE OF THINGS TO KEEP IN MIND AS YOU READ:

First, this book was written from my experiences over twenty years of ministry, but the experiences mentioned are predominately from the last two roles I have held overseeing Family Ministries in both Michigan and North Carolina.

Second, I occasionally make mention of people in my past and present ministries who illustrate the principles or ideas in this book. In some cases, you will see an asterisk following their names, indicating that those names have been changed to protect the privacy of those individuals.

INTRODUCTION:
AN UNPLANNED JOURNEY

I have a confession. When I entered full-time ministry, I never really considered partnering with parents to be high on my priority list. I was committed to ministering to kids. Someone else could take care of the parents, right? On top of that, it wasn't long before I'd witnessed and experienced the pain of dealing with overly protective or critical parents in my ministry. From the parent who thought I only worked on Sundays to the parent who expected me to be on par with Jesus, it was easy to adopt a defensive approach to the parents I interacted with.

With those things in mind, I never saw the importance of expending energy to incorporate parents into my thinking and decisions. Typically, the average week of creating environments for kids and students provided me with enough to do. I didn't have time to add in communicating with and resourcing parents as well. I was barely treading water from week to week as it was. And what's more, why would I want to open myself up to parents, knowing that I might be criticized at some point?

Fifteen years ago, I was forced to discover some solid answers to these kinds of questions. What I discovered wasn't what I was expecting, but I'm forever thankful for where those answers have taken me.

I know that partnering with parents can seem daunting and overwhelming, but I promise you that it's one of the greatest ways to reach and equip the next generation. In fact, let me be so bold as to say it this way: If you're not prepared to partner with parents, it's very likely your success in ministry will always be limited. So come on a journey with me and see why partnering with parents will increase your effectiveness in reaching and equipping the next generation for Christ. You won't regret it.

WHERE I'VE BEEN

I'm not from around these parts. I grew up in the bustling suburbs of London, England. A number of years ago, I moved to Ann Arbor, Michigan. Previously, I'd been living and working in London as an insurance consultant while volunteering as a youth leader in my local church.

I had grown up outside the church. But thanks to my friend Andy Unwin, I was invited to an incredible youth group that forever changed my life. By the age of eighteen, I had accepted Christ at a youth workers' convention and was excited about pouring into the lives of young people. Looking back now, I realize that not only was God calling me to a new life in Him, He was calling me into full-time ministry. It took another seven years to respond to that calling. But along the way, I took some small steps as a volunteer; investing in kids just as some incredible adults had done for me in the years before. Over time I couldn't escape what God was calling me to, but I didn't quite know where to start. I didn't know, that is, until I spoke to Byron Porisch.

Byron was a 30-year veteran youth pastor who'd just been called to a large church to rebuild a struggling youth ministry that was once thriving. When I asked him for advice on where to start in pursuing God's call on my life, he gave me some incredible counsel and wisdom. Then he asked me a question that would change my life drastically: "What if you moved to the States, and worked with me? I can show you how it's done, and maybe we can help you with your tuition?"

That day, when I asked Byron for his advice, I never would have dreamed that I'd be changing careers and countries within a few months. It was a crazy idea, or was it? I arrived on a plane from England as a fresh-faced, twenty-something Englishman with a plan to intern with Byron for four years while studying youth ministry at a local Christian university. (Who in their right mind would agree to intern for four years? A fresh-faced Englishman, I guess). At the time, the university didn't offer a youth ministry degree, but rather a family life education degree. It was the closest thing to what I hoped to study, but I didn't really know what the degree program was all about. I was a little deflated that I couldn't study youth ministry, but I determined that my best education would come from being in the trenches of youth ministry with Byron anyway. In hindsight, I'm thankful for this "plan B degree" that forever changed my thinking on how best to reach and equip the next generation for Christ. It's also what brought me into contact with "Prof. Ben."

I met Ben Freudenburg in the second year of my internship and studies. He arrived on campus straight out the trenches of family ministry and had written a book called *The Family Friendly Church*. At the time, his book was already a few years old, but very few churches were even thinking about how to implement the kinds of things written on its pages. However, he'd been living and breathing family ministry for many years. He had a clear philosophy and was practical in his application.

Professor Ben is a pioneer in the family ministry movement. Much of his work has shaped the landscape of how churches can effectively reach the whole family. He was one of the first people to ask questions and provide answers about how church workers could continue their investment in kids while also employing a family-friendly strategy that empowered and equipped parents to be the primary influencers in their child's faith journey. Every class with Ben forced me to constantly evaluate how I was engaging parents in my ministry and how I could best equip them to continue the faith conversations and invest in their kids at home. How every calendar item, event, and program needed to consider parents first, rather than as an afterthought. Ben's vision was to see parents as our primary ministry, and everything else would flow from there.

By the end of my four years with Byron and Ben, I had learned a great deal. Perhaps the greatest thing I learned was that the church is called to partner with parents to reach and equip the next generation. I had concluded that much of my ministry would only be putting out fires if I didn't invest in parents just as much as I invested in the kids I saw each week. And I was absolutely convinced that the days of running a "silo" ministry—seeing my ministry as the predominant way to effectively reach children and students, and disregarding the role of parents or the importance of other ministries within the local church—could not continue. I could no longer send parents the unspoken message of, "Drop your kids off and leave it to us." Though many parents saw it as my job to raise their kids in the faith, I came to see that it was my role to engage those parents and give them a new vision, strategy, and the practical steps to take.

WHERE WE'RE GOING

As a leader, your effectiveness in reaching and equipping the next generation for Christ will be greatest when you partner with parents and see them as co-laborers for the Kingdom. It doesn't mean changing how you do your ministry entirely, but it will mean weaving some principles for partnering with parents into your existing day-to-day ministry. And that's actually great news for me and you. So many books give us ways to do ministry that are specific to a particular context and require us to clone our ministries after them. My hope is that after reading this book you can keep your ministry identity intact while more effectively partnering with parents and reaching the next generation for Christ.

It's also my hope that your church's governing body and the other leaders in your church will read this book. Not only will it help them see the need to give greater focus to partnering with parents, but it will also help them find strategic and practical ideas to implement this philosophy and strategy into the life of the whole church. As a children's, youth ministry worker, or key volunteer, take the time to grab a coffee with the influencers and decision makers in your church and talk with them about the thoughts in this book. It just might be a game changer for them too.

Chapter 1

THE NEED FOR PARTNERING

HINT: IT'S NOT ABOUT YOUR MINISTRY.

I grew up in England. As a kid, I was always enthralled by the sport of rowing. Every year around Easter, I would sit in front of the TV and watch the Oxford and Cambridge Boat Race. These incredible teams would work together to be the first along four miles of The River Thames in West London. The event is a huge deal on the British sporting calendar and is often watched by over two hundred and fifty thousand[1] spectators along the riverfront. Most years this race is hotly contested and usually provides a tantalizing finish in the last mile, with the honors switching between Oxford and Cambridge[2] from year-to-year.

There are usually three components that make for a winning rowing team. First, the team needs great strength and endurance to last throughout the entire race. Second, it's the rowers' efficiency in moving the oars in the water that helps the boat glide seamlessly through the water. Third—and perhaps most important—is the synchronization of the team. They have to work together in perfect unison so each oar hits the water at the same time and in the same way.

So what does that have to do with reaching and equipping the next generation for Christ?

9

Many churches today are out of sync when it comes to the way we approach children's and student ministries. While some of the oars may be working to propel the team forward, others are going into the water at odd angles or not at all as they try to deal with the most pressing concerns of the moment. They do this by recruiting and resourcing staff and volunteers based on those most pressing needs and not based on winning the race over the long haul. As a result, these ministries are falling behind.

For the most part, churches tailor their services and programs based on the felt needs of the people coming in their doors. Whatever is the latest and biggest problem will get the most attention and investment. As a result, we tend to give most of our time, energy, and resources to issues kids are struggling with in the moment rather than helping them to prevent those issues from coming up in the first place. Don't get me wrong. Investing in children's and youth ministry programs to meet the real and pressing needs of modern day families is important. It's something the church has done extremely well, but there needs to be something more.

HELPING PARENTS WIN THE RACE

Let's be honest. Parenting is a scary prospect and isn't for cowards. Headlines are continually dominated by suicides, bullying, addictions, and the advancement of an overly sexualized culture. In recent years, we've also seen greater pressure for parents to succeed financially as the world has walked precariously through pandemic and recession. The demands on the modern family have left many parents with limited time and resources to raise their kids, and they're looking to the church to help them.

Many parents are living in constant survival mode. Some are facing the realities of adolescence. They're watching their kids struggle through a multitude of potentially life-altering issues and feel completely inept at dealing with a fast moving youth culture. Parents are watching the race get away from them, and they're not sure how to catch up, much less get out ahead.

As I sat in a local coffee house writing this chapter, I saw a friend who is the senior pastor of a nearby church. I asked him how his church was doing, and his response confirmed my premise: "What draws people to most churches is crisis and kids. You've either got to meet a need that someone is facing or give them a place that'll be good for their kids." While we both agreed there are many additional reasons why a family might choose a good church, ultimately their choice will be swayed by whether their felt needs are being met and if there's a quality children's and youth ministry. A family will tolerate a mediocre church service if they feel their kids are having an incredible experience in the children's or youth ministry. In response, churches have improved their youth and children's ministry programs to attract parents who are desperate for help.

In a parenting seminar called, *Generation 2 Generation*[3], Dr. Jim Burns points to the foundations of youth ministry in the local church today. Many churches adopted an approach that was developed out the success of Young Life and Youth for Christ in the 1970s. From there, as Michael McGarry asserts in his book, *A Biblical Theology for Youth Ministry*, "Youth workers were largely resourced by Youth Specialties. Mike Yaconelli and Wayne Rice began producing resources to equip churches and youth workers through the ministry of Youth Specialties in the early 1970s."[4] Churches saw the great success of parachurch organizations and their ability to attract greater numbers. Now, for over half a century, we've seen a greater level of investment in youth and children's ministry as churches have recruited qualified ministry workers, bought the latest curriculums, and created exciting ministry environments for kids. In a similar timeframe, we also began to a shift of responsibility from parents to church ministries. In his book, *Connecting Church and Home*, Dr. Tim Kimmel concedes that,

> Little by little, parents began to sub-contract the spiritual heavy lifting to the professionals at church (and parochial schools). Feeling like this base was adequately covered, they could concentrate their attention on providing a better lifestyle and creating some fun memories. The parents' job shifted to offering occasional biblical sound bites and a full-time commitment to overseeing their children's spiritual report cards.[5]

In my experience, the church that provides a great children's and youth ministry will attract and keep the greater number of families. As I've talked with parents over the years it's been interesting to hear why they've chosen a particular church. Many have been honest enough to say their choice was not for themselves, but to get their kids engaged in a children's or youth ministry that would help their kids connect to other Christian kids and grow in Christ. At a previous church, one mom told me, "The worship service here is not what we enjoy, but we love the youth ministry here and we want to see our kids get plugged in. If they love it here, we'll get past our own preferences."

KEEPING A STRAIGHT LINE

As you read this, you might be wondering, "Is he going to to drop the hammer on children's and youth ministry? Is he about to say that meeting a family's needs is a problem? Is he against churches creating engaging environments where their kids can learn and grow in Christ in a way that's developmentally appropriate?" Certainly not!

I, too, want my kids to be part of vibrant children's and youth ministries. I want them to drag me to church and talk my ear off on the way home about how God has captured their hearts because of what they heard and experienced at church. I want to hear them tell me how they served, and how their lives were changed because of it. I want them to experience what I experienced all those years ago growing up in England, where my heart was opened to the gospel because of an incredible youth ministry. I want them to have other adults invest in their lives like John Powell, Patrick Horgan, Roger Gammon, Kate Dean, and Tim Lee, the people who invested in my life and helped me find Christ in the midst of a messy adolescence.

I believe in children's and youth ministries to the core of who I am. But that's only one side of the boat. And when you only use the oars on one side, you just go in circles. You have to work the oars on both sides of the boat to make any progress. Vibrant children's and youth ministries must be synchronized with partnering with parents to reach and equip the next generation for Christ.

There will always be a need for the church to provide outstanding ministry environments for children and youth. But there's also a need to partner with parents at the same time. In the past few decades there's been an imbalance in how much time we've spent responding to the immediate needs of kids compared to the time we've spent investing in and preparing parents as the primary influencers in their child's faith journey. If you don't agree, just look at the job postings for children's and youth ministry positions. Most likely, you'll find little to no emphasis on partnering with parents. And when it is mentioned, it'll probably be a vague reference at best.

Over the years, I have been struck by this imbalance at a number of national conferences who have a "family ministry" emphasis. So often, the message to "partner with parents" is there, but seldom do I hear the practical steps to partner effectively. Rather, they default back to talking about the nuts and bolts of what we, as children's and youth workers, do with our kids and students. And while what we do is extremely important, if that's all we focus on, there's a gigantic piece missing that has astronomical and eternal implications. But let's be honest, in most of our churches, we are measured by the usual metrics of attendance, how many salvations, baptisms, etc. They are all good measurements, but how do we measure what goes on in the families? How can we measure how well our investment in parents is impacting the spiritual journey of kids? We can survey families and involve them in giving feedback, but it takes more work and is not as easy to measure the impact of partnering with parents. Attendance is still the standard by which many of us are measured, but it does not mean we should cast the biblical vision to partner with parents and find ways to measure our impact.

Formerly, I would get frustrated about this disparity, but the longer I spend in ministry, the more grace I have to realize that all of us are still trying to figure this out. Even the "experts" are still learners. I am one of them. I used to be frustrated with church leadership who did not "get it," but I am coming to realize it's up to me to lead up and provide a clear vision and strategy for partnering with the whole family.

With that said, partnering with parents needs to be woven into the very fabric of what we're doing in our children's and youth ministries. The most successful churches will balance it with providing kids a great, Gospel-centered experience. When that happens, they become part of a team that successfully moves things forward.

Heading for the Right Finish

So we don't miss the most important point of all, let's be clear that partnering with parents and providing effective ministries to children and youth are not just about helping our kids get through the challenges they'll face in childhood and adolescence. Our ultimate goal needs to always be reaching and equipping them with the Gospel of Jesus Christ. It's that foundation of faith that will best enable them to navigate through the inevitable challenges of life.

Rick Lawrence makes a similar point in *Jesus Centered Youth Ministry:*

> Up until now most of us have been like overworked pruners in a fast growing orchard. We scurry around trying to cut off the bad fruit we see around us… The truth is, as kids come to know Jesus more deeply and begin to abide in him more deeply and begin to abide in him as the 'root' of their life, their fruit will change. They will be transformed 'by the renewing of [their] mind' (Romans 12:2). We won't have to run around cutting off rotten fruit.[6]

I wholeheartedly agree. And I'd like to weave in an additional thought: Helping kids and students know Jesus more deeply happens best when parents are empowered to be the primary ones equipping their kids' for their faith journeys. It's not that you and I stop sharing the Gospel with kids or providing excellent environments for them. It's that we need to intentionally focus on setting up parents to become the spiritual heroes in their kids' lives. Equipping parents to raise their kids with a Jesus-centered foundation will result in their kids being better equipped to face the challenges of today and tomorrow.

Getting All the Oars In

One of the most common objections I hear from other children's and youth pastors often goes something like this: "I know I need to partner with parents, but what if they don't want to partner with me?" It's a fair question. Many parents are disengaged, having a "drop off" mentality where they see us as the experts who'll save their kids. But in some cases, they're simply too busy keeping up with life. Partnering with you and me is often just one more thing to add to their already hectic schedules. What's more, many of the families we serve are already consumed with helping their kids deal with some kind of pressing issue. In those cases, we need not to see parents as disengaged so much as being engaged somewhere else, and it's our role to help them bring an urgency and attention to engaging with their children's faith journey.

It's our job to sound the alarm; to alert parents to the difficulties their kids may face now and in the future. Doing so is a key to grabbing their attention. The more parents can understand about what's ahead, the greater the likelihood they'll make a priority of investing in their child's spiritual journey now. But our role is not simply to scare the life out of parents by exposing them to the potential struggles their kids will face now and in the future. Rather, it's to educate them regarding those issues. Doing so is often the catalyst for parents making changes in the way they raise their kids in the faith.

For any good communicator, it's crucial to get the audience's attention at the beginning of a message by stirring up a sense of need. It's no different when you're dealing with parents. Some of us are grabbing the attention of children and students on a weekly basis, but we don't realize the need to grab the attention of parents by sounding the alarm on the issues their kids are facing. Once we have their attention, it's more likely they'll take time to listen to someone like you or me who can partner with them and equip them to equip their children with the life-changing Gospel.

In *Barna's Gen Z* research, 99% of all church leaders agreed that parents ranked as the number one influence in their child's faith development. Parents are with their kids substantially more than you and me, and therefore have a greater overall potential to influence their children's faith journey. It's the way God designed it to be. If we're lucky we might get a couple of hours a week with the average child or student who attends our church. Between mealtimes, car journeys, vacations, school events, and hang-out times, imagine how many more hours the average parent has compared to that. Imagine how many more teachable moments that provides parents compared to you and me. Think of what would happen if we were to support parents by equipping and empowering them to make greater use of those times to instill faith into their kids' lives. You and I have limited potential when we focus only on what happens at church. However, there is massive potential when we emphasize what happens at home as well.

MOVING AHEAD ONE STROKE AT A TIME

"But how can I give parents practical help?" If you haven't asked that question yet, I'm sure you will soon. In my early days of ministry, I knew I was meant to partner with parents, but with the exception of a few authors and organizations, there were very few resources to help. There are still only few resources that provide practical "how to's" for reaching, equipping, and partnering with parents. Many of those that do exist are program specific and leave me feeling like I have to change my ministry and become a clone of some mega church in a totally different context. I often walk away from those kinds of resources feeling like they've provided very little in the way of "rubber meets the road" ideas, strategies, or steps.

This book is a practical "how to" that's not program specific. Whether you're full- or part-time in ministry or a volunteer, these ideas can be woven into your ministry at your own pace. I know I get frustrated when I read books or go to a conference that requires me to overhaul my whole ministry to make a new strategy work. The good news is that this book won't require you to do that. It might require you to add some components or reassign some resources, but you won't have to change everything you do. And here's the best news: you won't have to spend thousands of dollars on an expensive new curriculum, either.

The ideas contained here can be implemented as you read and as you lead in your context. The first part of the book is focused on understanding what's gone before us so we can look ahead to the future. So much of what we do in the local church had a starting place, yet many of us have come through the church and never sought to understand where we've come from or why we do what we do. The rest of the book gives insights and practical steps that can be implemented immediately in most contexts. As you read, take time to pause and consider how you can weave those things into your ministry. At the end of every chapter are questions to answer and action steps to take that will help you do just that.

That being said, a word of warning is also due: Don't try to change the world overnight. Begin with some easy wins and go from there. Changing the culture of a church and the mindsets of parents can and will take time. It's important that you take small steps as you solidify your thoughts on partnering with parents and then implement out of your convictions. Since there's still a potential for big changes in your ministry, it's helpful for everyone around you to experience one step at a time. That'll make a huge difference in the long-term. In my experience, change comes best by employing a strategy of small steps that make a marked difference over time. Not only are small steps easier to manage on your part, they'll always be easier for people around you to stomach.

A while ago, I sat down with a group of youth workers in a local restaurant as part of a networking meeting. As we enjoyed lunch together we began to discuss ideas and resources with one another. I always love hearing what other churches are doing and seeing what ideas I could use in my context. As we shared ideas, the topic of partnering with parents came up and we began to discuss ways to engage parents in our respective ministries. But as we navigated the conversation, it was clear to me there was a disparity in what we saw as partnering with parents. One youth worker clearly indicated that, for him, partnering with parents was focused on recruiting parents to help him with his ministry and involving them in his organization. While this indeed is a step to partnering with parents, it was obviously what his emphasis was all about.

Let me be clear. This book is not about providing you with ways to get parents to do stuff for you in your ministry or support your vision. Rather, this book is about helping you partner with parents so you can support them in pursuing a biblical vision to reach and equip the next generation for Christ.

A final word of note. As you read the phrase "partnering with parents" throughout this book, it's important to understand that I am referring to a number of key influencers in the lives of children and students. I am aware that many children in our churches today do not have a traditional family or parents. Many are raised by grandparents and other family members. In these instances, you can replace this phrase with "partnering with the family."

So, are you ready? Grab a cup of tea with me (remember, I am English), and let's dive into this together.

Endnotes

[1] https://www.visitlondon.com/things-to-do/event/8716237-boat-race.

[2] https://www.theboatrace.org/the-basics.

[3] https://homeword.com/seminars/generation-2-generation/.

[4] Michael McGarry, *A Biblical Theology of Youth Ministry*, (Nashville: Randall House Publications, 2019), 72.

[5] Dr. Tim Kimmel, *Connecting Church and Home*, (Nashville: Randall House Publications, 2013), 5.

[6] Rick Lawrence, *Jesus Centered Youth Ministry*, (Loveland: Group Publishing, Inc., 2014), 102.

[7] https://www.barna.com/research/children-faith-formation/ March 19, 2019.

IT STARTS WITH YOU

HOW YOUR EXAMPLE CAN MAKE OR BREAK YOUR ABILITY TO PARTNER WITH PARENTS.

It was a conversation that would forever change my marriage and my ministry. As I sat next to my wife Lisa, tears trickled down our faces, the once new couch we bought when we got married was no longer comfortable and was falling apart. In the past year, our torn and tattered couch had become a reflection of our lives in ministry. On this particular day the pain of loss only amplified the messiness of marriage and ministry.

Like many couples, we were navigating the immense pain of miscarriage. As tears flowed, I was struck by just how quickly my soft-spoken wife was able to articulate her feelings and emotions. In the past, I'd learned to wait for her to talk, and sometimes it could mean waiting a few days before I really heard and understood her heart. But this day was different from others as she talked openly about our grief and the pain of our loss. As we talked together, it was like the loss of our baby had allowed us to capture what was most important in our lives. C.S Lewis once said, "God whispers to us in our pleasures, speaks in our conscience, but shouts in our pains: it is His megaphone to rouse a deaf world."[1] That was true for us on this day. We experienced God's comfort. But we also experienced incredible clarity.

"If you never did ministry again, I don't think I would care." As the words came out of her mouth, I didn't feel the need to push back or clarify what she meant. I didn't need to look her in the eyes and wonder where such a thought came from. I didn't fall off the couch from a devastating surprise. I knew exactly what she was thinking and feeling. I instantly knew why she needed to speak in such a direct way.

The Problem

I had a dream job in ministry: build a ministry from the ground up, design it how I wanted, and share in the fruit of a fast-growing church plant. If you've ever been involved in a church plant, you know that it's easy to wear many hats; and if you're not careful, it's easy to sacrifice yourself and your family without realizing it. That was the case for Lisa and me. And as a result, the dream quickly became a nightmare. What was once a blessing, felt more like a curse.

The hard, but honest words Lisa spoke hit home as she shared her frustrations of being married to an overscheduled, unhealthy youth pastor. It wasn't like I didn't see it coming. Over many months, I had blurred the lines of ministry and family. I'd created an unhealthy ministry schedule in a church that was exploding with growth. My overscheduled ministry had become the enemy of my faith walk, my family, my health, and my relationships. We looked around and realized we had little time for friends. We were isolated and alone. In the midst of a miscarriage, we were broken, discouraged, and our dream had been lost. We had crashed, and we were hurting.

The Need

No one ever thinks it'll happen to them. No one sets off in ministry planning to burn out. In the midst of it all, part of me was in denial. But another part of me knew there were things I needed to change. I'd been to conferences that told me to set boundaries and create balance. I knew some simple changes would make all the difference, but I was allowing the complexity of ministry to lead the way.

I couldn't blame the church. And even though I often blamed the people who were leading me, it was ultimately my fault for not defining the boundaries for my life and ministry more clearly. Every time I said "yes" to being at church more than was really needed, was time missed with my family. It took the hard but necessary words of my wife and the pain of a miscarriage to shake me back to reality. It was time to dream again. Time to create a vision for our family and ministry.

In the next year, I embarked on a journey of change that would result in a change of priorities and a change of churches. It was extremely painful to leave a church and group of people I loved. But I've never regretted taking the opportunity to rediscover what it means to make my family my first and primary ministry. I wish I could tell you that I've gotten it all figured out since then, but there are still times I realize that I've said "yes" to too many things. In fact, I've come to the realization that I have the propensity to be a "speed addict" as John Mark Comer describes himself in his book, *The Ruthless Elimination of Hurry*[2]. Fortunately, Lisa and I have learned to communicate better and see the signs of imbalance quicker. We've also been learning the importance of having clear vision and values for our own family, along with some long-term healthy practices. Family and ministry are often moving targets, so having a clear vision and healthy practices is essential. It hasn't been easy, but it's been worth striving after a healthier balance between family and ministry, even if it's meant taking some big steps of faith as a family. Ultimately, we've seen God bless both our family and ministry as we have sought his best for both.

The Answer

The way you invest in your own family will significantly affect the fruit of your ministry. To be more specific, you can't expect to see fruit in your ministry if there's no fruit at home. Let that reality sink in for a moment. It's easy to agree with it on the surface. But consider the ripple effect it can have in our lives and ministries.

Whether you're single or married, young or old; whether you're a rookie or have years of experience, your example will always speak louder than your words. If you truly want to attract and influence other families, the vision, priorities, and foundations you live out in your family must be distinctly different from the harassed and stressed world that you live in. I'm not saying you have to be perfect at it. But, we live in a world where talk is cheap. Over time, our ability to influence others is diminished when they see that our lives are in conflict with the message that we preach.

THE CHALLENGE

> Keep putting into practice all you learned and received from me—
> everything you heard from me and saw me doing. Then the God
> of peace will be with you (Philippians 4:9).

Imagine being one of the Christians in Philippi reading Paul's letter and remembering all he taught you. And, as if his teaching wasn't enough, you remember his example, too. It was his teaching and example together that let him say, "Whatever you heard from me is only part of the picture. Look at how I lived the truth too. Then, go and live it out yourself. You know it's the real deal."

Despite a little embellishment on my part, I think you get the idea. And here's what's so imperative to understand as it relates to partnering with parents: Partnering begins with how you invest in your own family first. Your teaching and instruction must be seen in how you personally live out your faith in your family. It needs to be an overflow of who you are. That's what'll make you a lighthouse for the watching world.

The way we invest in our own families is the most attractive reason for parents to follow our leadership. As parents engage in defensive battles related to their kids, they're looking for hope and direction from people who are successfully defending their own families. It stands to reason that you wouldn't make a financial investment with someone who has a track record of wasting his or her own money. In the same way, parents won't listen to you and me if we're not passionately pursuing a healthy family life ourselves. That's true for us if we're single or married and whether we have kids or not. Our example is the greatest tool we have to influence the people who are looking to follow our lead. Your investment in your family will have a greater long-term affect than some of the most innovative programs and ministries you can create. And, if you fail to invest in your own family first, there's far more at stake than just your ministry.

THE GOAL

If you talk to my wife Lisa, she'll affirm that I'm not Jesus. The good news is that's not the goal. It's not about being perfect (or appearing to be perfect). It's about authentically pursuing God's best for your family. In fact, I would go as far as to say the "rough edges" of your family will put others at ease when they realize you're just like them. Who wants to follow a perfect family anyway? I sure can't keep up with that standard.

I have a confession. In my early years of ministry, I used to think that I could not make an impact on other families, unless my own was in good order. I even wrote a blog post and made the case that investing in our families has to happen before we can leave a lasting impact on our ministries. At the time, I thought this was a clear-cut argument that everyone would be quick to agree with. After a few emails and a couple of comments, I came to realize how naïve it was to assume this was a given for the readers of my blog. Thankfully, no one can find my naïve blog post any longer. With that said, I've come to see a dichotomy between those who pursue balancing family and ministry and those who don't. I've observed those who've ensured the health of their families came first, and as a result their ministries were healthy, too. On the other hand, I've watched some people sacrifice their families for ministry at a huge cost, not only to their families, but to their ministries and their long-term effectiveness as well. My hope for you is that this chapter will prompt you to consider the health of your family (or future family) and consider the example you're setting for those you lead. Remember, you won't be perfect, rather an authentic leader who is leading others in pursuit of God and a healthy family life.

THE BIBLE

Ministry is a calling and requires us to make sacrifices at times. However, a quick look at Scripture will help us balance that out. In 1 Timothy 3:1-3, Paul instructs Timothy regarding the requirements for church leaders:

This is a trustworthy saying: 'If someone aspires to be a church leader, he desires an honorable position.' So a church leader must be a man whose life is above reproach. He must be faithful to his wife. He must exercise self-control, live wisely, and have a good reputation. He must enjoy having guests in his home, and he must be able to teach. He must not be a heavy drinker or be violent. He must be gentle, not quarrelsome, and not love money.

For a young leader like Timothy, it was crucial to hear Paul explain what to look for in leaders who would leave a lasting legacy and have an effective ministry in the church. Timothy was in Ephesus. And in the Ephesian church at that time, many of the current and potential leaders were being sucked into unhealthy habits by the Greco-Roman influences of the day. The culture was extremely narcissistic. Status and power were sought at any cost. Many church leaders were falling into sin and accepting false teaching. There was plenty of opportunity for the leaders of that day to get swept away by a sea of self-focus and allow the waves of unhealthy habits to swallow them up, even where their families were concerned. Consequently, Paul knew that leaders would need to be solid in their faith and conduct, including in the ways they managed their families.

Take a moment to consider the world you and I live in now. It's not all that different in terms of the priorities and values Timothy had to deal with in the church at Ephesus. We still see leaders fall into the traps of status, power, and striving for significance. Consider some of the other traps you and I fall into as we try to minister to those around us:

- **We focus on pleasing people.** We live to make others happy instead of pleasing God first. We say "yes" to everyone and everything and feel ashamed at the thought of saying "no." In the meantime, we become worn out and ministry loses its joy and excitement. We run on empty and give our families our leftovers, if there's anything left to give.
- **We build platforms.** We attempt to build a platform of influence for ourselves and leave little to no room on the platform for Christ. We're constantly fueled by the accolades of success and trying to make a name for ourselves. It's possible we are envious of those Christian celebrity speaker and pastors, secretly wishing we have their platform.

- **We mistake our identities.** We base our identities on what we do rather than who we are in Christ. Rather than being confident in the person God has made us to be, we're caught up in the position we hold.
- **We break boundaries.** We don't say "no" to ministry needs, yet we constantly say "no" to time with and focus on our families. We see it as the easier route, expecting our families to be more understanding than our senior pastors or congregations.
- **We lose our devotional lives.** We let our study time for ministry become a substitute for our personal devotional time. We let reading God's Word and applying it personally and practically get replaced by lesson preparation for the benefit of others.
- **We ignore worship.** We let the corporate worship experience become a distant memory as we look to serve others and ensure that everything depends on us. We encourage families to sit together in church, but our own families haven't had that experience for a long time.
- **We aren't fully present.** Rather than shutting off our technological gadgets at strategic times, we convince ourselves that every phone call, text message, email, and social media request has to be answered right away. We send our kids and spouses the message that the outside world is more important than they are.
- **We ignore our physical health.** We don't take time to exercise, and we let food become a source of comfort that leads to health complications over time. We lack energy and always feel like we need more sleep (which is very possible). We're told that the body is the temple of the Holy Spirit, yet for some of us it feels like the temple is crumbling.

Do any of these traps speak to you right now? At some stage or another, these have all been true for me, and I still have to depend on God's grace and truth to navigate through them from time to time. As leaders, we are under constant pressure and temptations. It's so important to confess and acknowledge the areas God needs to be invited into.

So, where do we go from here? With God's help, we work on our own faith and family, then we look to impact others around us. After giving Timothy the list of prerequisites for church leaders, Paul builds the bridge between who a person is at home and who he or she is as a church leader: "He must manage his own family well, having children who respect and obey him. For if a man cannot manage his own household, how can he take care of God's church?" (1 Timothy 3:4-5).

And there it is: the crucial connection between how we minister to our own families at home and our ministry to the church. It's also the foundation for how we partner with parents. If you and I don't know how to invest in our own families first, we can't begin to understand how to invest in others' families.

GAME SUMMARY

The way you invest in your own family will significantly affect the influence you have with parents.

PRACTICE DRILLS

Use the following action steps to help you implement what you've learned in your life and ministry.

1. In the next 24 hours, take time to journal about your faith, your family, and your ministry. How do you think others view your family? Is your family life and your personal walk with God a light in the darkness for others to follow? How do you match up to the kind of leader Paul told Timothy to look for in 1 Timothy 3? What has God been bringing to your attention as you've read this chapter?

2. Identify one or two areas of your faith or family life that need attention. Create one attainable goal for each of those areas that'll help you bring them to the forefront of your ministry.

3. Contact two or three key people who'll give you an honest assessment of how well you're prioritizing your family and your walk with God. Set up a time to talk about what they see, and ask them to hold

you accountable for making positive changes in any areas of potential growth they see.

4. Ask a close friend, mentor, or accountability partner to discuss any unhealthy motives or habits you can relate to. Ask that person to walk alongside you as you work to eradicate those things from your life and ministry.

5. Create a vision statement for your family. If you're married, be sure to include your spouse in the process. A good vision statement paints a picture of a hoped for future. Take time to pray and dream about it, and make sure your statement reflects a healthy balance between God, family, and ministry.

Endnotes

[1] C.S Lewis, *The Problem of Pain* (San Francisco: HarperOne, 2015), 91.

[2] John Mark Comer, *The Ruthless Elimination of Hurry* (Colorado Springs: Water-Brook, 2019), 8.

Chapter 3

Build a Unified Team

Work past your own hesitations and understand the parents you're partnering with.

We're called to be on the same team as we reach the next generation for Christ. But let's face it; parents can sometimes be scary figures to deal with. Partnering with parents can be painful and can leave the strongest of leaders with scars and insecurities. Is it any wonder why so many youth and children's workers avoid certain parents or avoid parents entirely?

If you've been in ministry for a while, you probably have some stories and possibly some scars that have been caused by a parent lashing out. In my early days of ministry, it was relatively easy to avoid dealing with parents, as I was an intern who lived under the protection of the full-time paid guy. If I ran good programs and communicated well, parents would be happy with me—for the most part. But it wasn't long before I was under the microscope and under the scrutiny of a few parents who didn't like a decision I'd made. It's painful to sit across the table from a parent who was questioning why I wasn't doing more for the ministry, and their child in particular. I soon began to see parents as the enemy, with my default being to be on the defensive. And if the best defense is offense, it didn't take long until I went on the attack. I eventually discovered the pain of being told, "Parents are talking, and they don't like what you're doing with our kids." My quick rehearsed comeback was, "Well, I don't like what *they're* doing with their kids…" But like I said, that was in the early days. For the most part, these days, my quick defensive comebacks stay in a dusty vault somewhere in my head.

I'm learning that in the midst of criticism or failure, it's easy to point out the flaws in a particular parent and blame them for the damage I had to "clean up" in their kids' lives. Every time I went to a conference I would hear (and share) stories of problem parents and hurt feelings. At times, my encounters with parents caused me to wonder if ministry was even worth the effort. Sadly, my wife Lisa would hear some of the rants that came out of my mouth in those moments of hurt and frustration:

> These people care about sports more than they care about Jesus. Why don't they make their kids' faith journey a priority? They want me to lead their kids to Christ, yet they don't seem to be doing anything at home.

I could go on and on, but you get the point. I'm not trying to get you all riled up. Rather, I'm just trying to help you know you're not alone. Many of us have stories of conflicting with parents in our ministries. If you don't already, you probably will at some point. You and I are broken people with insecurities, as are parents—who are on the same team. As a team we're called to reach and equip the next generation for Christ. The devil would love to create team disunity since he knows it's effective in stifling the vision that we, as a team, need desperately to hold onto.

UNDERSTANDING THE PLAYERS

"David" had only been in ministry for a short time and was nearly ready to throw in the towel when I spoke to him a few years ago. As a young married guy in a new church, he'd arrived with a great deal of zeal and purpose. Within a year, he was tired and depleted by a small group of critical parents. As a new leader, he admitted he made too many changes at once, and also acknowledged that his communication skills were not the best. Before he knew it, parents were talking to his pastor and he was beginning to hear about their frustrations second hand. The pressure was mounting and it seemed an insurmountable task to win back the favor of the parents.

If you're like David or me, there are days when you just want to disengage from the pain of partnering with parents. But in those moments, it's essential you and I face a reality: Our effectiveness in reaching and equipping the next generation is limited only if we fail to understand parents and involve them in our thinking, planning, and implementation. By shifting our focus from seeing parents as opponents to become teammates to win alongside of, we increase our effectiveness in ministry.

While I can't control how parents act or react toward me as a leader, I've discovered that listening to them and finding understanding is the best start I can make. However, while we might be good at understanding children and students, many of us aren't very good at understanding parents. Part of the reason for this is we don't take time to truly listen to parents.

Before I had kids of my own, I often found it challenging to understand where parents were coming from. I didn't take time to listen. And honestly, I didn't see the importance. It wasn't hard for me to relate to David, since I used to be just like him.

During those years before Lisa and I started a family, I asked some supportive parents to become my "eyes and ears" and a sounding board for what I was thinking and planning. More than anything, I wanted to cut down on the potential for criticism by running ideas past parents first, but I also discovered some key insights from some honest and vulnerable parents. Many of these discussions gave me an inside track to the life of parents who came through our church doors every weekend. Then, when I eventually had my own kids, it gave me even greater insight to the joys and struggles experienced by parents. As I began to see parents differently, I began to minister to them differently. And the way I view parents today has greatly influenced my efforts and increased my effectiveness too.

READING THE ROSTER

For the remainder of this chapter, it's my goal to give you a snapshot of some of the parents in your ministry. While we can't talk about every kind of parent in your ministry, it's my hope that God will give you some greater perspective into their lives and the worlds in which they live. My hope is that if you see them as an opponent today, you'll see them as being on the same team tomorrow.

Distracted parents. First of all, it's imperative that we realize our perception of parents isn't always accurate. We see this best when we consider what it's like to walk a mile in their shoes. As I've leaned in and listened to the heart of parents, I've often found them to be more distracted than they are disengaged. They're either distracted by a plethora of competing priorities from work and home, or consumed with creating well-intentioned pursuits they hope will bring success for their kids. Their schedules are full, their attention span is short, and their energy is low as they try to keep up with work and family life. And where disengaged parents are often hard to reach, distracted parents can be won over. Begin by seeing parents as distracted rather than being disengaged, and from there take the time to truly understand the distractions and challenges they're facing.

Overwhelmed parents. Many parents are living in survival mode. In recent years, parents have been forced to make decisions that take time away from the family in order to pay the bills. A Pew Research study shows that over half the parents with children under the age of 18 find it a challenge to balance family and work.[1] The study confirmed that 74% of parents with children under 18 at least sometimes felt like they were too busy to enjoy life. In another study, 31% of parents said they always felt rushed.

In their harried situations, they don't know where to begin when it comes to investing in their kids, spiritually. But, most parents would never want to admit that to you and me. After all, people in the church are supposed to have it all together, aren't we? Even if a parent had a good role model growing up, there are many times he or she may wonder if what they're doing is making a difference. (I know this to be true for Lisa and me. There are times I've had to hold on to the words of my mentor, Ron, who told me to, "Stay the course and be consistent even when you feel like it's not working.") Overwhelmed parents need you and me to encourage them to stay the course rather than guilting them in some way.

Helicopter parents. The mark of a helicopter parent is one who hovers over their kids' lives every moment of every day in an attempt to see them be successful. If there's a way these parents could be seen as disengaged, it's in the way they prioritize their children's faith. They're so busy making sure their children don't miss out on opportunities to advance socially, academically, or in any other way the parents see as important, their child's spiritual growth can fall to the wayside. So often, it's not that they don't care, it's simply that they don't see the importance. They have great intentions but the wrong priorities.

Lawnmower parents. Close relatives to helicopter parents are the "lawnmower" or "snowplow" parents. (Depending on what your climate looks like, the snowplow parent might not translate so well—I spent fifteen years in Michigan, so snowplow works well for me). Essentially, the mark of this kind of parent is how they go ahead of their kids to remove any obstacle or threat from their child's path. They want to be there to support their kids and ensure their kids are well rounded and set up for success like a helicopter parent, but they take things a step further. They will go ahead of their kids to protect them from experiences that might actually be growth opportunities.

For the positive, both helicopter and lawnmower parents want to be involved with and actively participate in their children's lives. I've seen this to be true for over a decade, as much larger numbers of parents want to volunteer in the ministries their kids attend. They're also open and receptive to helping their kids grow in the faith. However, it's also possible for helicopter and lawnmower parents to be overly involved and stifling to their kids. In their attempt to give their kids the best opportunities for the future, they will help orchestrate and fill their kids' schedules with all kinds of extra-curricular activities that'll one day look good on a college application. Often, this kind of focus can lead to their kids not having ownership and a say in their future—or in their faith journey.

When we see ourselves as being on the same team as helicopter and lawnmower parents, we can offer them support and help redirect their efforts. Their intentions are good, and they want the best for their kids. It's up to us to listen to them, build trust, and then we can channel their motives into a greater focus on reaching and equipping their kids for the faith journey.

Single parents. According to the Kids Count Data Center, 35 percent of all children in the United States live in single parent families.[2] While that figure could vary depending on a variety of factors, the point is that many of the parents in your ministry could be single parents who are trying to manage a house, a job, and raising their kids to be happy and healthy. Given the load they carry on a daily basis, they already see you as a partner, but only in a partial sense. You're the one who gives their kids a place to go to and have fun while learning about God. You give them a break from their kids for an hour or two a week, allowing them to attend church or get their grocery shopping done while their kids are at youth group.

These are also the parents who may give you a hard time if you ever cancel youth group or take a break for a week or two. For them, it's a huge deal to find an alternative event to occupy their kids. Don't take it personally if they're abrupt with you at times. It's not that they mean to come across as self-focused or critical, they simply can't see beyond their harried life that's teetering on a tipping point. In my experience with single parents, there's often a story of regret concerning their kids that they carry around with them. The fact they're at your church is huge, since being at church with people "who have it all together" is a painful reminder of their struggles. A few years ago, "Kerry" shared with me how she always felt accepted and welcome at church, but personally, she struggled with the stigma of being a single mom at church. Since then, I've met many more single parents that have communicated the same struggles and insecurities.

Because single parents already see you as a partner in helping them with their kids, it's crucial that we help them see the greater scope of how we can be on their team. So often their schedule is the hardest part about being able to come alongside them, so it's crucial to over communicate the calendar and to ensure we offer them support at times when they're naturally and normally at church.

Parents with kids with special needs. In my time in ministry, I've never seen so many children and students with special needs as I've seen in the last decade. A number of years ago, I was at a medium-sized church with limited resources but a huge vision to minister to families with special needs. We decided to put a stake in the ground and create a ministry that would not only allow parents to attend church, but also a place where their kids could grow in their faith and discover a place to belong. It is perhaps one of the most challenging ministries to coordinate from my perspective. Not only does every child or student have very specific and unique needs, it is highly volunteer-intensive and requires a great deal of diligence, safety, and training. But it's so fulfilling! There are times I've been teary-eyed watching our children with special needs as they engage their peers and adult "buddies" in our children's and student ministries. I'm also moved when I see their parents (some of whom are single parents), who are steadfastly committed to them in every way. I try to imagine what their day-to-day world is like, and I can barely fathom how they cope. "But by the grace of God and his enormous strength," is what one parent told me a while ago.

As I've talked with parents who have children with special needs, I've come to realize that not only is their world constantly demanding, but many of them have not always seen the church as a place of support and hope. This makes my heart heavy. And, it should. The early days of special needs ministry were defined by a conversation with a mom who led a group for parents of children with special needs. She shared these valuable but heart-rending insights with me.

> We never have a minute to ourselves, and it's hard to invest in other key relationships when I have to be focused on caring for our child with special needs. We're always *that* parent with *that* kid. It's hard to come to church since many churches don't understand or know what to do for our kids and us. In twenty years, this is the first church where I've experienced this kind of care and concern. I wish we could have found a place like this for my son when he was young.

It's my hope that, as I have, you'll develop a heart for these families who traditionally haven't found a place to belong in most churches.

While I could go on with other categories of parents you and I see every week, for now I hope that what I have provided serves as a snapshot to get you thinking about parents and help you better understand their worlds. It's certainly easier to see ourselves as being on the same team with parents when we've taken time to listen more, learn more, and love more.

The Most Important Perspective

Of all the things I could say to you about parents, what I am about say is possibly the most important. They are the real heroes. Not you. Not me. It's them.

To be candid, I used to get caught up in the false idea that I was the hero to the kids in my ministry. How about you? You see, being in front of kids and students, coming up with exciting games and life changing messages can be an incredible aspect of what we do, but it's just the set up to further great things with their parents. How are we *really* setting up parents for success at home? Now, don't misunderstand me. Yes, we are hero of sorts in the eyes of kids, but our role is to guide the parent heroes and partner with them as they invest in their child's faith journey. When we see them as the real heroes in their kids' lives, and step aside from the spotlight, what we give our time and focus to will likely change. Is it time to move out of the spotlight a little? Or maybe it's time to move the spotlight a lot?

Unifying the Team

Being on the same team with parents isn't rocket science. There are some universal principles that go a long way to partnering with them and allowing them to see us as being on the same team. They begin with the simple actions of praying, listening, understanding, and involving.

Praying. Prayer is such a simple thing to do, but I've found that the busyness of ministry means I often don't take time to pray for the ones I minister to—especially parents. While I might make time to pray for kids, it has taken work to get into the habit of regularly praying for parents. And, as I've developed that habit, I've learned that I need to not only pray for parents as they raise their kids, I need to ask God to give me insight into parents' lives and wisdom to see how I can best support them. It seems simple, but it's incredibly powerful when you and I take time to seek God's wisdom.

Listening. Listening is a doorway to trust and partnering with parents, but sadly it's often disregarded in the busyness of our ministry schedules. When we take time to listen, we communicate care and concern for the parents who are on our team. It doesn't have to be a major undertaking. It can happen in the lobby of your church, or when parents pick up their children at the end of programmed ministry times. Asking parents about their week, how their kids are doing, and how you can pray for them is a great place to begin. If you're a leader of a ministry, it's essential you have volunteers that enable you to be free to talk with parents as they drop off or pick up their kids. You can't be so busy doing things with kids that you have no time to engage with and listen to parents. If you're a volunteer and don't have any other adults to hand responsibilities off to, it'll mean consciously balancing your contact time with kids and parents. Don't try to get to every parent every week, begin by seeking out one good conversation per week with a parent. Even one conversation each week will help you build trust and better understand the hearts of the parents you minister to. And here's a great question from my friend in ministry, Chris Sasser: "Our goal is to partner with parents. When we say 'we are here to partner with parents,' what does that mean to you?" Of Course, the answers will differ from family to family, but the most frequent answers I hear from parents are often one of the following types of questions:

- Who are they? "Help us understand our child or teenager better. There's so many changes going on with them I can hardly keep up with knowing who my child is becoming."
- How can we talk to them? "We need practical help in bringing faith into our conversations at home."
- What's happening at church? "We need good communication about how we can get our kids involved at church and in the community. Please make it easy for us to get information."
- What does their culture look like? "We need resources and education in better understanding the latest culture and trends our kids are walking through."
- What can our family do? "We need help with ideas for how to grow and serve as a family."

Learning. Not only will parents trust you when you listen, but you'll gain understanding that helps you see parents differently. In my early years of ministry, I spent too much time talking to parents, trying to show them what I knew. In more recent years, I've taken greater time to listen to and learn from parents, trying to get a better understanding of where they're at. Whether it's through a face-to-face conversation or through surveys, it's essential to understand parents' worlds and how you can support them as they reach and equip their children.

Involving. Earlier, I referred to recruiting some parents to be my eyes and ears in ministry. I wanted these parents to be sounding boards for my decisions, hoping they could help me avert poor decisions and improve what I was doing. But like many of my plans, I discovered that God had a greater purpose in mind. As I got to know and love those parents, they not only became the catalysts for some of my best ideas and helped me to avoid potential disasters in scheduling and programming, they became my allies, my advocates, and they gave me a better perspective on the things we discussed. Let's take a moment to consider some of those benefits to listening to, understanding, and involving parents.

We gain allies. When all is said and done, the most important aspect of being on the same team as parents is the result we all experience together. As we'll see in the chapter on vision, we're called to partner with parents to reach the next generation for Christ. When we work as a team toward this vision, we see greater things happen in the lives of children and students in our ministries. It means we have to swallow our pride at times, but some of the best solutions I've seen have come from the wisdom of parents who feel like they're part of the team and who sense a real ownership of what we're trying to accomplish together.

We gain advocates. No matter what we do, there will always be criticism from parents. Don't forget, many of them are harried, overwhelmed, and insecure (just like you and me). When we receive criticism, it's essential that you and I have a team of parents we can listen to and talk with about what we're planning and doing. The members of that team can become great advocates for us. As parents, they're well positioned to represent us to other parents who don't yet see the big picture or might have misunderstood our intentions.

Early on in my ministry journey, a parent misunderstood some decisions I'd made in the student ministry. In between church services, I had one of those awkward conversations with a parent who was clearly incensed with my decisions. As people walked by wondering why this mom had steam coming out of her ears, I politely smiled and nodded as she piled on a tirade of criticism. Fortunately, at that moment, one of my volunteer moms (who knew our plans very well) was walking by. I was able to stop her and ask if she could help me explain where I was coming from. I acknowledge that I probably hadn't done a good job explaining things, and needed her help. Not only was it a great day to have a parent volunteer on my team, it was also a great day for an irate parent to see that we were all on the same team together. Seeing the decision through the lens of another parent made all the difference, and it taught me the importance of having parents who would one day be advocates for me.

We gain perspective. Just being able to sit down with parents and talk through ministry plans has given me great insights into their world. There's been a few occasions when I've looked to make a change in the night of the week our high school large group was meeting on. Prior to these decisions, we surveyed as many parents as possible and recruited a small team of parents to help dissect the findings. Even though the surveys concluded a need to change, my parent teams have helped me see some of the tensions such a change would bring to certain families. By understanding these tensions, we were able to construct a good communication plan that addressed them ahead of time. By having parents' perspectives on this issue, it allowed us to diffuse potential conflicts and allowed other parents to see that we had considered their thoughts and feelings. I would never have seen those tensions on my own. Perhaps one of the greatest benefits of gaining parent input and perspective has been when programs have failed. If you are living by faith and taking healthy risks, it's only a matter of time that something will fail. It's been on these occasions (and there's been a few), when having a parent perspective and buy-in has been crucial. The "in it together" mindset will not only own the failure, there will be a team of parents committed to rebuilding and reworking until a good solution is found. Making huge decisions in isolation of parent perspective can be so much more efficient and cleaner, but it's a lonely and messy place to be when plans fail.

Partnering with parents begins with getting on the same team with them. But, it doesn't stop there. As you develop an understanding of their needs and the strengths they bring to the team, you'll build a team that can work together to do some great things.

GAME SUMMARY

The way we view parents affects the partnerships we develop with them. Viewing parents as being on the same team leads to greater effectiveness in reaching and equipping the next generation for Christ.

PRACTICE DRILLS

1. Take some time to journal your responses to the following questions: How have your experiences positively or negatively affected the way you view parents in your ministry? How does the way you view parents in your ministry shape the way you engage with them? How does it affect your ability to partner with them? How would your ministry be different if you had parents who saw themselves as being on the same team as you?

2. Divide a sheet of paper into three columns. In the first column, create a list of difficult parents in your ministry. In the second column, list any fears or struggles you're aware of that each of those parents is facing. In the third column, write down some ways you could encourage those parents regarding their fears and struggles. Take time to pray for each of the parents on your list and for God to give you wisdom in how to come alongside those parents.

3. List some of the places you most often see parents. For each of those places, identify one step you can take to free yourself up to listen to the parents you see in those places. If any of those steps require advanced planning on your part (such as having an adult volunteer who is able to take over with kids while you interact with parents) begin making those arrangements today.

4. Contact 3-4 key parents and ask them to be your "eyes and ears" in ministry. Meet with those parents, presenting a basic agenda of decisions they could help you think through and focusing on asking them questions rather than casting a vision. Aside from questions about specific decisions you're working through, ask questions such as:

- What are the major issues our parents are struggling with as they raise their kids in the faith?
- What would our parents want me to know about them or their kids, but are too afraid to share?
- How approachable am I to parents?
- What are we doing to help parents instill faith at home? What could we do better?

5. Take 15 minutes to pray for your parents today. Ask God to bring to mind those parents who could be struggling. Take another 15 minutes to send a note, a text, or an email to encourage those parents and let them know you're praying for them.

Endnotes

[1] https://www.pewresearch.org/fact-tank/2020/02/05/how-americans-feel-about-the-satisfactions-and-stresses-of-modern-life/.

[2] Children in Single Parent Families in The United States. https://datacenter.kidscount.org/data/tables/106-children-in-single-parent-families. Accessed August 10, 2020.

Chapter 4

CAST THE BIBLICAL VISION

THE IMPORTANCE OF HELPING PARENTS AND CHURCH LEADERSHIP SEE THE BIBLICAL CASE FOR PARTNERING WITH PARENTS.

I grew up outside the church. My parents and I only went to church for weddings and funerals. In fact, the first time I went to "church" on my own was when my friend and I decided to break in to steal some candy from the youth group candy stash. God has an incredible sense of humor since, just a year later, I was invited by a friend to attend that same youth group. Even though I thought I might be struck by lightning when I set foot back in that church, I said, "Yes." From there, I spent the next four years hearing about Christ and seeing an incredible example of God-honoring leaders who showed great patience with me. At the age of eighteen, I accepted Christ and my life was forever changed.

Fast forward many years. I was married to Lisa. I was in full-time ministry. We had a mortgage and the first of our three children. There I was, a pastor in a local church who had absolutely no idea how to raise my kids in their faith journey. No one had ever shown me what to do or what to say. Talking about faith was absolutely foreign to my parents. As a new father to little Emma, I desperately searched for advice, wisdom, and some keys to raising my kids with a solid faith foundation. I knew it was my job to invest in my kids first, but getting started was a lot harder than I anticipated. Over the years, I've come to realize that I'm not the only parent who's had similar feelings of inadequacy. I've also come to see that many parents have gone before me and made an eternal difference in the lives of their kids.

We Need to Capture the Vision

Most parents I meet don't know where to begin when it comes to raising their kids with a solid faith foundation either. In fact, many parents I meet don't even realize it's their God-given role to invest in their children's faith journey. This problem is amplified by the unspoken expectation many parents have that it's the children's pastor's role to equip their kids for a lifelong faith journey. Even if parents do know that it's their role to invest in their kids, many of them are often so overwhelmed with their work and extra-curricular family schedules they don't make time to invest in their kids. These are the parents I struggle with the most. They know their role, but they choose to make sports, academics, and personal fulfillment a greater priority than their child's faith journey.

Before we get parents on board with a vision for raising their kids in the faith, it's important that we understand what the Bible says about the part we play in pursuing that vision. If all we do is point fingers at parents, we're missing the big picture. We all have a role to play in accomplishing God's purposes for the children and students he's entrusted to us.

Deuteronomy 6:4-9 says:

Listen, O Israel! The Lord is our God, the Lord alone. And you must love the Lord your God with all your heart, all your soul, and all your strength. And you must commit yourselves wholeheartedly to these commands that I am giving you today. Repeat them again and again to your children. Talk about them when you are at home and when you are on the road, when you are going to bed and when you are getting up. Tie them to your hands and wear them on your forehead as reminders. Write them on the doorposts of your house and on your gates.

Picture this incredible and historic moment with me for a moment. After 40 years of wandering in a desert due to unbelief and complaining, Moses and his people arrived at a destination that should have only taken a short time to find, but God had other plans for them (Deuteronomy 1:2). As they stood there on the Plains of Moab, you can imagine their relief and expectation as they sensed this was a new beginning for a whole generation of people. The atmosphere of change was in the air and their waiting and wandering in the desert had finally come to an end. Imagine the faces of the people as they stood before Moses and waited for him to speak. This was it. This was the beginning of a new movement, a new chapter, and a new destination. The people were ready to hear from their leader, and they were ready to go the next mile in discovering God's new blessing. They were ready to take new ground and move beyond the failures of the previous generation. As Moses began to speak, they were hanging on every word, every instruction, and every command. What they heard would be groundbreaking and would guide their whole nation for generations to come.

It's critical that we understand the importance of Moses' words to his people at that time. It's also essential we understand the importance of those words to us today. That's what the rest of this chapter is about. Moses' words are relevant to you and me as we look to improve upon the past and forge ahead in influencing the world for Christ. Much is at stake in reaching and equipping the next generation for Christ.

Looking back over the past few decades, the lack of synchronization in our churches regarding our approach to children's and student ministries—along with a consumer mentality—has allowed us to lose sight of a biblical vision for reaching the next generation. Many leaders in the church have fostered a "leave it to the expert" mentality (albeit unconsciously at times), and many parents have played along with it. Let me give you an example.

Emily's parents understand the cost of having a child play on a traveling team, but they also see how well Emily is developing as a soccer player. Her soccer coach, Drew, is a great inspiration. He clearly loves the sport and has a great pedigree, having played collegiate soccer and won numerous titles at the semi-professional level. As for school, Emily's parents couldn't be happier with the teachers who invest in her academics each day. Moving houses and changing to one of the state's premier school systems was well worth it. Between Emily's soccer schedule, youth group activities, and her parents' careers, there's little time for them to keep up with all the academic changes.

Emily's parents are thankful to have a team of support for Emily as she navigates transitions from elementary school into what seems like a weird (and somewhat scary) middle school phase. In particular, they've seen her becoming more autonomous, and becoming more aware of a fast-changing culture, and for them technology is just, well, overwhelming. Her parents are especially thankful for the church they've been attending. They love being part of a church where their kids are loved and receive engaging teaching that's relevant to them. In particular, they are thankful for Emily's youth pastor. In their eyes, he understands teenagers so much better and seems to have a greater connection with them. Emily's parents see that he knows the Bible better than they do and knows how to explain things to Emily in ways she connects with. Even when Emily attended children's church, her parents thought the leaders there just had a better way of engaging with and speaking to the kids about Jesus than they ever could. The children's workers just knew what to say and what to do in a far better way.

Does that sound familiar? Emily's parents are one of the many types of parents you and I meet every day. They're busy and stretched and looking for "experts" to come alongside them as they raise their kids. While this makes sense in some areas, God never intended parents to leave their child's faith development to someone else. But sadly, many of us in church leadership have often affirmed this approach by creating silo programs that are solely focused on children and students with little to no consideration for parents—either in terms of how we can equip them or how we can involve them. It's as if we've said, "Leave it to us, we'll teach your kids what they need to know. Give us an hour a week, and we've got you covered. You see us as the heroes, and we will step into that role for you."

Now, I don't think most of us intentionally communicate that parents are unimportant or mean to leave them out of the picture, but our modern-day church culture has often caused it to happen. In addition to pushing parents to the sidelines, it's also created an impossible task for children's and youth pastors to accomplish. And for those parents who are intent on investing in their child's faith journey, they feel alone as they look to the church for help.

WE NEED TO UNDERSTAND THE VISION

God's vision and design for raising the next generation is for it to be done as a partnership between parents and the church. It's time that we come back to that vision and design; the one that Moses gave his people many centuries ago. As we look back at some of the failures of the past, it's essential that you and I take new ground as we partner with parents in raising their kids in a solid faith foundation. To do that, let's look more closely at those great words Moses spoke to the waiting generation in his day. Let's take those words and build a bridge of application to our world today.

IT'S FOR EVERYONE

Listen, O Israel! (Deuteronomy 6:4).

For years, I had missed the importance of those three words in the context of this passage. As a pastor who works with families, my default has always been to focus on the role that parents play in impressing God's commands on their children. It's the part I want parents to get. It's the part that allows me to emphasize their role and take the responsibility off of my shoulders. However, that only works if I ignore those first three words. You see, when Moses gave this command it was for a whole nation and people, not just one targeted segment. Its central message wasn't just for parents, and it wasn't just for the church. It was a message for the whole faith community to commit to and to live out for generations to come. And the same is true for us today. Reaching and equipping the next generation for Christ depends on everyone in our faith communities. That includes parents, you, other church leaders, the college grad who just moved back home, the empty nester couple who now loves to travel. Everyone has a part to play.

When I was growing up in the England as a kid, all of my neighbors knew me. If I set a foot wrong, there was an expectation that they would look out for my parents and put me straight. They would also be the ones to encourage me and laugh with me. Every parent on my street was involved in supporting the kids in the community. (They also used to get involved in some killer soccer games with my friends and me, but I digress). Here's the point: In our world today, the idea of families and communities partnering together has quickly become distant, consumer driven, and shallow; the "in it together" mindset is being lost. No one seems to want to take responsibility. It's always someone else's job to take care of the kids.

As leaders in the church, part of our role is to cast the vision that, when it comes to reaching children and students, we're all in this together. It's a responsibility for the whole church to take on. It's a call to ensure that everyone (even your church janitor) understands they have a role to play in reaching and equipping the next generation for Christ. "Listen, O Israel" was for a whole people group, and it's for your whole church to grasp today.

In the churches where I have served, baptisms or dedications are often times when the pastor charges the congregation to support parents as they commit to raise their children in the Christian faith. During such ceremonies, the pastor asks the congregation to commit to supporting the child and his or her parents; at which time, everyone stands up and declares, "We will by the grace of God." However, it's possible for people to forget what they just agreed to as soon as they sit back down. Therefore, it's important that we continue to cast the vision for an "in it together" mindset whenever we can. We can't just talk about it at baptisms or dedication and hope that it'll stick.

It Begins With Me ✕

> And you must love the Lord your God with all your heart, all your soul, and all your strength. And you must commit yourselves wholeheartedly to these commands that I am giving you today (Deuteronomy 6:5-6).

Just as we discussed in an earlier chapter, it's crucial that God's commandments be written on our own hearts first, so we can be a light to those we lead. Perhaps the most powerful advice I was ever given by a mentor was to ensure that my own faith walk was strong and authentic, first and foremost. If God's truth is impressed on my own heart, it will authenticate all that I teach and train in my own household. That's why I've also told parents the best gift they can give their children is an authentic faith that shows a love for God and for others. It's vital that you and I encourage parents to grow in their faith and promote other ministries in the church that will be a support to parents. For example, even though I have never overseen small groups, I've constantly promoted small groups and Bible studies to the parents I meet. When parents are growing in their faith through small groups, I know that'll have an effect on the teaching their kids will receive at home.

It's Ongoing

> Repeat them again and again to your children. Talk about them when you are at home and when you are on the road, when you are going to bed and when you are getting up. Tie them to your hands and wear them on your forehead as reminders. Write them on the doorposts of your house and on your gates (Deuteronomy 6:7-9).

One of the challenges parents face is how to communicate God's truth to their children. I've read a lot of books for parents that have lofty ideas and present wildly complex systems for instilling faith in my children. I've been in church ministry for over two decades and even I often walk away from them feeling overwhelmed or confused as to where and how to begin. That's where Moses' words can help parents see that passing on the faith to their children doesn't have to be rocket science. It's simply about grabbing onto the teachable times and creating intentional moments with our children. (I'll explain more of what I mean by that later.) It's the same thing Jesus did with His disciples. Some of their greatest lessons came as they walked and talked and engaged in life together. That's great news for parents and for us.

As we communicate to parents the vision for passing on the faith to their kids, it's important that we distance ourselves from lofty, ambiguous ideas and offer them practical and specific ways to accomplish the task. After all, it's the practical and specific that parents will be most likely to implement. I'm not asking anyone to water down what they communicate, but it's essential that it's relevant and practical to a busy parents whose time and resources are limited.

There are natural and normal opportunities that parents have to introduce faith into conversations with their kids. By taking advantage of those opportunities, parents can create a culture in their homes of having faith-talks throughout the day. Over time, such talks become natural and normal for the kids and parents, both, and feel less forced. Deuteronomy 6:7-9 outlines some of those opportunities for us. One commentator summarizes them this way: "By means of a figure of speech Moses uses opposites—sitting and walking, lying down and rising up—to suggest that any time is appropriate for instruction in the ways of the Lord.[1] While the times and places Moses provides need some contextualization for our families today, I've found that they create an outline of sorts that can be useful for parents as they consider how to invest in their children. Let's take a look at each of those times now.

When you're at home. Even the busiest family will have times when they're all gathered around a table for a meal. Granted, as kids get older and extra-curricular activities are in full force, having time to gather around the dinner table gets harder to come by. But, when you do find the time, it's a great opportunity to thank God together for his blessings and debrief the day—what Brian Haynes refers to as "God Sightings."[2]

When you're on the road. Growing up in England, I remember times walking down the road with my mom or dad as we went to a friend's house or to the soccer field. However, here in the States, my experience has been that there are fewer sidewalks and everything's far away (at least by English standards). So, I apply this idea to my time in the car with my kids—no matter how short a distance we travel. My oldest daughter's previous school was about one mile from our house, so we could literally walk along the road. However, if you know my pokey little girl, you understand that getting going in the morning has always been a challenge, and a car ride was usually needed. Even on the short journey to school each morning, we shared prayer requests for the day and prayed for each other. And at the end of day, when I picked her up, it was always a great time to debrief her highs and lows and talk about what God might have been teaching her during the day.

When you're going to bed and when you're getting up. Right from our eldest's birth, Lisa and I created a habit of reading the Bible and praying with our kids before bed. There are some days we do better at it than others, but those times have become part of our family's culture that are hard to miss or forget.

There was a time, after a long day out and returning home late, I decided to cut out our Bible time and simply pray with my two girls. Oh my goodness! You would have thought I had grounded them both for two weeks. They created such a stir and gave me such a guilt trip for not reading together that I had to give in. Now that they are older, it's part of what they do as a daily practice.

Here's the brilliant thing about encouraging parents to take those teachable moments at bedtime: For the most part, children (students included) just seem to be more spiritually sensitive and a lot more open at bedtime. It's almost like the Holy Spirit has softened them up and helped them to tune into Him in greater ways. One night as I kissed my five-year-old good night, she asked, "Daddy, if God loves all people, why does He allow some people to go to Hell?" In the busyness of the day, it's possible that kind of question would have never even been asked (or answered). But as the day was winding down and my daughter was settling for bed, her heart opened up—as did a great opportunity to speak into her life.

I used to think that passing on the faith would require me to implement lofty ideas with a great deal of planning and struggle. Sadly, many parents I meet have a similar view on what's required of them. They either try too hard, implement something their kids dislike (some might use the word "hate"), or give up altogether. Just before the birth of my oldest, I sought advice from parents whose kids were older and who I thought had done a good job passing on the faith. One parent I spoke to named Deb shared some wisdom that immediately alleviated my fears and gave me instant confidence that I could make a difference. She said,

> First of all, it's by the grace of God that He used me. And second, it's all about the teachable times and bringing faith into everyday situations, times, and places.

If you have kids of your own, take Deb's advice and use the teachable moments to make faith stick with your kids. Encourage the parents in your ministry to do the same. Her counsel is simple, yet powerful. I've experienced the benefit of creating teachable times in my own household with my kids. You and the parents to whom you minister can do the same.

IT'S INTENTIONAL ✕

"Tie them to your hands and wear them on your forehead as reminders. Write them on the doorposts of your house and on your gates" (Deuteronomy 6:8-9). Throughout the centuries, Jewish families have taken these verses quite literally. They tied small boxes containing words from the Torah to their hands and foreheads and also placed copies of the Torah on their doorposts.[3] But many commentators would agree that Moses didn't intend these verses to be applied in this way. Rather, he was communicating the principle of creating intentional traditions, monuments, or milestones that would keep God's truth at the forefront of families' priorities. Such practices become reminders of God's grace in the life of a child as well as roadmap of growth for a family to follow. In the chapter on Milestones, we'll look at how to do these things more specifically. But, perhaps the most important thing for parents to understand is that creating intentional moments, traditions, and experiences gives their children goals to look forward to and markers to look back on as they grow. By helping parents understand this, we encourage them to integrate a culture of faith into their family's lives rather than separating faith from everyday living.

WE NEED TO CAST THE VISION

Influencing church leadership to embrace a vision of reaching the whole family is critical. After all, your leaders set the direction of the church. And if a church employs you, it's likely you'll have to get them to buy into partnering with parents. But that's not always easy to do.

In a previous church, a senior leader promised me he was committed to reaching parents just as much as reaching their kids. However, after being there for a year, it was clear that what mattered was producing a knock-out youth ministry program that would bring more families to the church. The idea of expending energy to partner with parents was foreign and was seen as a drain on creating an incredible youth ministry. It certainly wasn't written in my job description. And in hindsight, I wish I'd done more in the interview process to ensure that partnering with parents was a priority. However, despite this disparity in vision, it didn't prevent me from finding ways to cast the vision to those over me and build consensus about partnering with parents.

Influencing our senior leaders is a slow process and takes a lot of work, but it's essential if we're going to successfully incorporate partnering with parents into our ministries. Let's finish out this chapter by taking a look at some healthy ways to go about it.

Focus on your job description first. It doesn't matter if you're a volunteer or paid staff, the leaders in your church see your primary responsibility as investing in children or students (or both). We have to remember that the idea of partnering with parents and the titles of "next generation pastor" or "family ministry pastor" are foreign to many leaders in the church. They are more familiar with the traditional titles of "youth director" or "children's ministry director." We also have to consider that there's a certain way children's and youth ministry has been done over the years. Therefore, it's essential that we gain influence first by doing a great job in the roles we were hired to fill. In previous churches, it has taken me nearly two years to establish a ministry that gave me the credibility to add in a greater focus on partnering with parents. However, that didn't mean I couldn't lay groundwork as I went.

Pursue the healthy conversations. Part of our role is to constantly find ways to passionately communicate to those who lead us, the need and vision to partner with parents. However, in my experience it's crucial to pursue such conversations in ways that are positive and that advocate the reasons for partnering with parents, as opposed to criticizing what the church is missing out on. In pursuing healthy conversations with the decision makers in your church, keep in mind that they're usually managing multiple people, plans, and ideas. So, ensure that you come prepared, and give it time.

Own the vision. When you own the vision yourself, you'll be able to communicate it not just out of your head, but from your heart. And, that'll greatly increase your ability to persuade those above and around you. But owning the vision means more than just being passionate. It means being thoughtful as well. Learn to articulate why it's essential to partner with parents in a sentence of two. Provide a biblical basis along with some practical examples of how partnering with parents is more effective. Take the vision and begin formulating it into a plan. If you don't feel ready to do those things yet, I hope that by the end of this book you'll have found some good ideas to get started with.

Have a strategy. One of the greatest shortcomings in my early days was not having a good strategy that other leaders could support. While many were quick to agree with the idea of partnering with parents, none of them had really ever thought through what that truly meant. For many of them, it seemed as if we were already partnering with parents. Communicating a strategy that includes a timeline and specific steps showing a progression of implementation is crucial. But continue to work on meeting the goals your senior leader has set for you as well. Even with a good strategy, they're ultimately going to measure your success by the program you develop for kids. We will talk about an effective strategy later in the book.

Share stories. A story of life change is always going to be the most effective way to cast vision with leaders in the local church. We all want to know one thing: Does it work? Providing stories of how partnering with parents is making your ministry more effective and how it's helping parents to be more effective is crucial. Once, I created an event for parents and children to celebrate and serve together over Christmas. The event itself was nothing out of this world, but it was a great way to help parents and children focus outwardly during the Christmas season. Following the event, we posted a number of photos of kids and parents serving together and even created a quick video to show at our Christmas Eve services. The following week there were countless replies to the photos from proud parents who thanked us for the opportunity to serve with their children. Being able to cast vision with key leaders through the replies of those parents was simple, but effective. Sometimes it's the low-hanging fruit of posting photos or a video to social media that paint a picture of a ministry that desires to partner with the entire family.

Request "stage time" in big church. Depending on your context, it may not be difficult ask for promotion or "stage time" in your church. Personally, I've had to work hard to gain opportunities to cast vision and promote the ministries I have led.

Even though there are always many events to be promoted and that require stage time, it doesn't mean we can't ask for it, too. As long as you don't come across as a whiney kid, you might be surprised at the opportunities that come your way. One of the best tips I can give you is to provide a steady drip of short stories of life change to your lead pastor. Not only will it keep him updated and excited, you might be surprised how many times your stories will show up in a sermon, or in a conversation with key stakeholders.

Train the team to be vision carriers. Probably one of the most effective ways to cast vision is to ensure you inspire and equip your team to be vision carriers. Essentially, it will mean have a simple and clear vision and strategy they are inspired by, but also a vision that is easy to repeat. Additionally, it will mean revisiting the vision regularly and ensuring you ask them to share stories about the ministry with everyone they know. When you have a "grass roots" team of adult volunteers (and parents) who are equipped to share vision and stories of life change, you will be surprised how many doors open for you. You won't need stage time.

Commit to the long haul. One of the greatest ways to help your leadership capture the vision for partnering with parents is longevity. The longer you stay, the greater your influence. In my experience, it usually takes about two years to establish relationships, figure out how things work, and develop a track record to point to before you have the clout to recommend changes to what's expected of you. Depending on the culture of your church and the leaders who make the decisions, it'll take time to make progress toward partnering with parents. Perhaps the most effective step you can take in that direction is to get to know the influential leaders in your church and give them the opportunity to get to know and trust you.

So many leaders have an unrealistic outlook on what it takes to cast vision and bring change in a church. They seem surprised when people aren't fully on board with their new vision and incredibly innovative ideas. It's not that the vision is off or that the ideas aren't solid. It's often a matter of too fast, too soon. The ability to influence others—especially those over you—comes by forming trusting relationships, and such relationships are developed over the long haul.

GAME SUMMARY

In a world of competing priorities, parents need a biblical, compelling, and practical vision for reaching and equipping their children in the faith.

PRACTICE DRILLS

1. Identify one or two Bible passages that support your vision to reach the next generation through partnering with parents. Take time to reflect on those passages, writing down any insights you find. Take time to pray, asking God to help you know how to use those insights to cast the vision of partnering with parents to others.

2. Contact three or four key leaders in your church who could help you cast vision and influence others with the vision to partner with parents. Set up a time with each of those leaders to share your heart and cast the vision.

3. Give copies of this book to influential leaders in your church, and ask them to read it. Tell them you'd like to hear their thoughts about the ideas it contains, and set up a time to meet with them and discuss those ideas.

4. Identify ways outside of formal meetings in which you can continuously cast vision to parents, volunteers, and church leaders. How can you weave the vision for partnering with parents into your regular communication pieces? Where could you go that would provide you the opportunity to interact with the people you want to catch this vision? How do you demonstrate the vision of partnering with parents in the way you interact with the people in your church?

Endnotes

[1] Ted Cabal, Chad Owen Brand, E. Ray Clendenen et al., *The Apologetics Study Bible: Real Questions, Straight Answers, Stronger Faith,* (Nashville: Holman Bible Publishers, 2007), 277.

[2] Brian Haynes, *Shift—What it Takes to Finally Reach Families Today,* (Loveland: Group Publishing, 2009), 44.

[3] Donald F. Ackland, "Deuteronomy," in *The Teacher's Bible Commentary*, ed. H. Franklin Paschall and Herschel H. Hobbs, (Nashville: Broadman and Holman Publishers, 1972), 118.

Chapter 5

COMMUNICATE
STRATEGICALLY

IDEAS FOR HELPING PARENTS HEAR YOU OVER THE NOISE.

The event you've been preparing for months is nearly ready to kick off. With the focus on kids and parents coming together to celebrate and to serve, this could be a game changer for your church. There's no end to the opportunities for you and your numerous volunteers to connect with parents, not to mention the relationships that'll be built between the parents. The auditorium has been decorated by you and a hard-working team of volunteers. Everyone's in place. There's an air of excitement and expectation as your team gets ready to see the excited faces of kids and parents come through the doors.

Fast forward an hour. Parents and kids are present in body, though not necessarily in spirit. As you survey the large room, you're keenly aware that you and your team nearly outnumber the group of participants. Inside, you feel far from celebrating, but your feelings aren't immediately noticeable to those around you. As you look around the room at the volunteer team, their faces display a look of forced excitement at best, deflation at worst, and an unspoken question: Where is everyone?

The drive home is filled with more questions as you reflect on the event and the lack of participation. The conversation in your head goes something like this:

Really? Why didn't they show up? Don't they care about their kids? This was in the church bulletin for four weeks. We even sent home a flyer with all of their kids. What's the point of partnering with parents if they don't want to partner back? Sometimes I think I care more about their kids than they do!

At the stoplight, you're ranting angrily to yourself and at God as you find yourself utterly deflated. For a moment you find some levity as you catch a glimpse of the person in the car next to you as they stare inside your car looking for the person you're spewing to. But alas, they conclude you're crazy and drive away quickly. You conclude that you might be as well, and that it's the parents who are the cause of your craziness.

PARENTS ARE ON INFORMATION OVERLOAD

Does this situation sound familiar? I can't tell you how many times I've put my heart and soul into an event only to have a dismal turn out. Unfortunately, this is par for the course in ministry. But it's a course that doesn't have to be repeated with great frequency. Whether it's an event for kids, for their parents, or both—it's imperative that you and I realize we live in a world where parents are bombarded by hundreds, if not thousands, of messages every week. It's a phenomenon I call, "promotion dilution." I don't know if anyone has coined that phrase before, but it's one that I use a lot. So, if you've never heard it before, you can say you heard it first from some British guy.

Promotion dilution occurs when our churches attempt to promote too many events and programs at a given time. In our charge to promote everything we're doing, nothing really gets highlighted. Instead, the message behind every event and program is watered down as it competes with all of the other events and programs we offer. The fact is, people tend to gravitate to what's promoted the most and talked about with the greatest focus.

Consider how much promotion dilution is occurring for the parents of the kids and students you're trying to reach. They live in a world of constant communication as individuals, companies, schools, and churches vie for their attention and participation. Your church is one of thousands of competing voices. I only have to look at my own life to see how this plays out.

First, there's the plethora of paperwork my kids bring home from school. Then, there's the junk mail from companies offering deals that seem too good to be true. Even in the digital age, we still seem to get so much paper! On top of that, my inbox is jam-packed with emails from teachers, soccer coaches, dance instructors, (not for me, I don't dance), and my favorite stores offering "the best deal ever." And then there's a lawyer who keeps emailing me from some far away country offering millions of dollars in exchange for my personal information. And that's just my personal email account! I currently have over four thousand unopened emails that, at one time, I set aside to read later. (Most of these are promotional emails, but if yours is one of them…sorry about that.) Social media doesn't help either. These days I seem to miss half the updates from friends and family. I got to the point where I had to turn off the notifications on my phone. And, speaking of phones, mine is in silent mode on a regular basis. Every evening I get calls from telemarketers or some recorded political call.

I could go on and on. We live in a fast-moving world where communication is constant. And by the time this book is in your hands, there's likely to be some new communication device that makes it even faster.

If you took a moment to consider just how much information and promotion comes your way on a weekly basis, you might just blow a gasket! The same is probably true for most of the parents you communicate with. We've already established that parents are harassed and harried; now add in the thousands of competing messages for their attention and participation. You're one of thousands of other voices vying for the attention and participation of parents in a world of promotion dilution. It's naïve to expect parents to get your message quickly.

Whether or not your church has a formal bulletin or video announcements on the screens as they enter your church, it's likely that you have a particular place in your church that's the primary distribution point for getting information to your church family. But, even if parents do read the church bulletin Sunday morning, they've likely forgotten what they read and misplaced the bulletin (or just threw it out) by the time Monday rolls around. What's more, sickness, sporting events, and family getaways mean that typical attendance is about twice a month for a lot of families. Therefore, they only get to see your information about twice a month (and that's assuming they even read the announcements).

We have to accept that we live a world in which parents receive constant communication from a multitude of sources. Whether it's the local school, the sports coach, a corporation, or some shady guy in another country, you and I are in competition for the attention of the parents we're trying to reach. And the competition is stiff. So, what are we to do?

SAY THINGS MULTIPLE TIMES IN MULTIPLE WAYS

Even though we have stiff competition for the attention of parents and kids, there are some ways we can engage them and assist them in making faith a greater priority. We can learn a great deal from the research and techniques marketing companies are already employing, while also leveraging our unique identity as the church to get an open door to a parent's focus and commitment.

In the world of sales and business, experts maintain that it requires many "touches" with a single person before that person buys a product.[1] That means a salesperson or business has to connect with and present information to people several times before those people become customers or clients. While we're not sales people, we have to accept that we live in a consumer driven world where the goal is to get a person to buy into a product or service. Our brains have been trained to tune into a consumer driven world in the way we engage with media and marketing. While the church isn't merely a product or service, it's still imperative that we recognize how people's brains are wired and how they'll process and respond to the information we send them. That means we'll have to communicate to parents with multiple touches as well. We might not like this reality, but it's unlikely that the average parent will get your message the first time around.

I love using email marketing software that tracks exactly who has opened a message and how many people have opened it in total. It's sometimes been amusing to speak to that one parent who claims they never saw an email, yet I can clearly see that he's opened it. I've also come to realize that I'm that parent at times. A quick look at an email on my phone, and I've soon forgotten that I even saw it, much less whether I replied to it or not. It's like the email was invisible. My own humbling experiences as a parent are helping me realize that an effective message needs to be in front of someone several times before they really "see" it.

Perhaps one of the most startling statistics I've discovered is that only 25.17 percent of non-profit emails are actually opened[2]. If you think that's bad, you should feel sorry for the vitamin supplement business (yes, there's an email marketing category for them). Their open rate is a measly 15.03 percent. While the open rate for many of us is better, we must accept that nearly three-quarters of parents will never even give our messages the time of day.

While communicating a message with multiple touches is necessary, it's also imperative that we communicate in multiple modes. (This is where we hope to catch the parents who do not open email.) With the onset of social media, I used to hear that many companies were likely to abandon other "outdated" modes of communicating with their potential customers. However, as I survey the landscape of sales and media, I see that companies are still using multiple avenues to communicate with their potential customer base. Once, a popular car manufacturer showed up in my social media feed offering me the chance to win one of their incredible cars. Since I was a youth pastor at the time and had the junkiest minivan on planet earth, I saw this as my only viable opportunity to own a brand-new car with all the bells and whistle on it. Without hesitation, I gave them all the information they asked for, and I even entered my wife's name too. (She wasn't impressed.) In the following months, we both received multiple emails from this car company along with glossy brochures in the mail. I regularly see this company show up on my social media feed along with the commercials I come across on TV and the radio. (Yes, I'm one of those people who still listen to the radio.) The point in all of this is that not only are companies communicating to me multiple times, but they're also communicating to me in multiple ways. But why do they communicate in different modes?

Not all parents are wired the same when it comes to communication. Some don't particularly care for technology or use it well, preferring to talk in person or receive a physical mailing. Others don't care for printed postcards, letters, or even phone calls, opting for email or text messages instead. You and I have a wide bandwidth of parents that consume information in a wide variety of ways.

A number of years ago, I came to realize that I was expecting parents to want to communicate in *the way I preferred*. Rather than promote things through a variety of means, I was gravitating to what I liked best. In the process, I was narrowing my audience reach and missing out on getting pertinent information into the hands of parents. If we want to have parents commit to our events and programs, it's crucial that we accept the need to get beyond our own preferences and communicate in multiple modes and at multiple times.

MANAGE THE FREQUENCY OF YOUR COMMUNICATION

"Is there a possibility of over communicating with parents? Will they tune you out if you send them too many messages?" These are valid questions I get asked. The concern is well founded in our world of promotion dilution. Simply stated, there's a balance to be found. Just as multiple focuses can easily lead to promotion dilution, it doesn't take much for a parent to feel they've heard your message so many times they can ignore the communications you send them in the future. Worse yet, is the possibility of them feeling like you're harassing them, which you definitely don't want to do. While multiple modes and multiple messages are essential, it also takes strategic management of the frequency with which we communicate.

I wish I could tell you that managing your communication is an exact science, but I've found that every community and church culture responds differently to the frequency of communication. Right now I live in a fast-paced community that's full of high-achieving parents whose kids are following in their parents' footsteps. In this kind of context, I can get away with a greater frequency of communication compared to other places I've served. Perhaps the most helpful piece of advice I can give you on this is to just ask the parents. Seek out three or four "go to" parents whom you trust to give honest feedback. Ask them to evaluate whether you need to adjust the frequency of your communication and in what way. Ask them to reach to a broader spectrum of parents to gain vital insights too.

Given that people move houses, and change email addresses and cell phone numbers, it's possible that you don't have current information for contacting parents. In my context, every new family registration and every event is an opportunity to gather information from parents. It's at registration you can let them know what to expect in terms of communication. It also helps gain both buy in and trust from the parents and shows them you're taking them into consideration.

One summer we had two large events back-to-back—a weeklong camp held at our church and an all-church picnic—that allowed us to engage with a massive number of parents. Some of them we already communicated with regularly. Some of them only knew about us through the church bulletin. (I guess it does work sometimes.) At both these events, we offered cards for families to fill out and enter to win some brilliant prizes. From these two events we were able to add numerous families to our regular communications lists.

No matter what your context is, it's important to space out your communications appropriately. It makes them feel less annoying and more helpful to parents. Here's an example of how I have endeavored to space out communications in the past:

Regular Communications

- Twice-yearly brochures to all parents with vision, programming, and calendar overview—Typically given out in twice yearly parent meeting/ parent training events.
- Quarterly calendars of upcoming and notable events—given online
- Monthly emailed newsletters or ministry overviews
- Weekly text message updates and reminders (linked to social media)
- Weekly social media updates
- Weekly parent take-homes for children's ministry

Special Event Promotions

- Promotional postcards given out 3-4 weeks ahead of a special event
- A short promotional video 3-4 weeks ahead of the event posted on social media (if this is in your skillset)
- Weekly social media updates starting 2-3 weeks ahead of the event
- Weekly email updates 2-3 weeks ahead of an event (spaced a couple of days apart from social media updates)

- Information included in our monthly parent newsletter
- Text message reminders sent the week of the event

"Seriously? You do all that?" you ask. Yes…and no. That's the ideal scenario and it depends greatly on what resources and skillsets you have. Sometimes, it will depend on the season in ministry too. For now, use it as a framework and ensure you contextualize it with your culture and environment.

If you're creating an event that's appealing to parents and their kids, it's far more likely that you'll have greater success with attendance if you increase the time and resources you give to promotion ahead of the event. While I can't guarantee you'll need to expand your church facilities to accommodate a huge turnout, my experience has shown me that promotion through multiple communication modes, over multiple times, with a strategic schedule always beats a bulletin announcement and an email. While it takes a lot of work and intentional planning, I'm convinced it's well worth it.

Provide an Opt-Out

Now that you have started thinking about changing your job description to "communications coordinator" let me encourage you to take two crucial steps: Provide an opt-out process and help parents get all the pertinent information in one place. Your parents need to know how to opt-out of your communication. Not only is it required as a regulation[3], it's also important to give parents the choice to unsubscribe if they are getting too much communication from us.

Create a Parent Hub

Where is the one place where new and existing families can get up-to-date information on calendar, resources, articles, and next steps for your ministry? When parents can't find that one email from you that's buried in their inbox with offers to win brand new cars that every youth pastor dreams about, they need to know there's a place to find it. Where is your parent hub? (*The Parent Hub* is actually what I named ours at a previous church.)

Build Relationships With Parents

I wish I could say that was it, but there are some more essential components that are worth reminding you of and pointing you to. So, before we continue, take a deep breath and remember that you don't have to implement everything all at once. Be thinking about how you can weave one or two ideas into what you're already doing.

While the world of marketing has moved toward a repetitive, diversified, and strategic plan, it also understands the importance of relationship. It's the game changer when it comes to getting your message across.

Good communication allows us to knock on the doors of parents. It's relationship that lets us in. When personal relationships with the families you work with are combined with multiple touches and multiple modes of communication that are managed strategically, your voice will begin to stand out. Your ability to get parents to show up to that incredible event or for them to make your children's ministry program the highlight of their child's week is deeply tied to relationships.

Relational investment builds trust and influence with parents. Parents will give their time and resources to leaders in the church they know and trust. Your relationship with parents is the greatest way to build a bridge to them owning and participating in the vision to reach and equip the next generation. It does take some time and requires a long-term view, but it can also lead parents to a long-term commitment to partnering with you in investing in their child's faith journey.

The Benefits of Investing in Relationships

In a world of sleek promotion and bottom-line sales goals, there's a great shortage of people who genuinely care these days. Even many of our school teachers and coaches have become too focused on meeting test scores or securing wins to the detriment of genuinely caring for kids and parents. We live in a world so focused on results that it neglects the need for relationships. When you and I take time to invest in relationships and have caring conversations with parents, we stand out from the noisy and impersonal crowd. Consider these other benefits:

- When you take time to talk face-to-face with parents about how to engage their child in simple faith conversations at home, you're investing in that child's faith journey.
- A personal invitation to an activity or event through a phone call or hand-written note can have a much greater effect than an impersonal email.
- Emails can be made to feel more personal with a quick in-person connection ahead of time.
- One or two conversations per week with parents can add up to greater overall engagement and commitment through the course of a year.
- When you create space in your schedule for face-to-face time with parents, they'll be more willing to create space on their calendars for ministry events and programs.

A common statement in children's and youth ministry circles is: "I know I need to partner with parents, but I'm so busy doing ministry with their kids that I don't have time to build relationships with them too." Not long ago I had someone say to me, "You're a family ministry guy now, of course you have time to partner with parents." But in reality, I've been building relationships with parents long before I took the role as a family pastor/next generation pastor. Doing it really doesn't require spending a lot of extra time. One brief, caring conversation at a time is all it takes.

How to Increase Your Face Time With Parents

When parents can look you in the eye or hear your voice on the phone, it's more likely they'll give your ministry greater focus and commitment. Let's take a look at some ways to better get in front of parents and build relationships with them.

Find time and make time. Take a look at when the parents in your ministry are naturally and normally around. For many of us, Sunday morning presents the greatest opportunity to meet and get to know parents. For others, it might be at a midweek program. In the past fifteen years, I've made it my goal to free up myself as much as possible on Sunday mornings and at the end of midweek events so I can meet and connect with the parents of the kids and students I'm ministering to. In fact, on any given Sunday morning it would be easy for anyone watching me to accuse me of being lazy and not having anything to do. I spend a lot of time standing around the lobby and hallways drinking coffee and engaging with parents. Sounds like a great job doesn't it? However, this is completely intentional on my part. It gives me the opportunity to have strategic conversations with the parents of kids I'm trying to reach and equip. Whether you're paid staff or a volunteer, it's essential that you find ways to free up yourself and make time to talk to parents. Allowing ourselves to get overly consumed with ministering directly to kids can often mean we're unavailable to engage in meaningful conversations with parents. If that describes you, consider how you could delegate a responsibility to free up yourself to engage more with parents.

Divide your time. Most of us are employed by or volunteer at churches that prioritize investing directly in kids' lives. And, frankly, that's what we want to be doing as well. The idea of using our time to talk to parents as we watch kids arrive and allow them to pass by creates tension for us at times. It also has the potential for creating tension in others. For those who don't understand the importance of partnering with parents, they might think we're giving up vital opportunities to invest in kids as we stand around and talk with their parents.

Practically speaking, though, I've had to make the choice to seek out two or three parents each week to talk to and encourage, knowing that in some way I'll feel like I'm missing out on contact time with kids. What helps is having a broad view of my ministry. It allows me to be confident that my investment in parents is an investment in the whole family. That's a view that all of us need to have. Yes, it's still important that we invest in the kids. But, it's imperative that we give time to their parents as well. If you're in a large church environment, consider what the effect would be if other staff members and volunteers were to each choose one parent to talk to and encourage each week. Imagine what the consequences of those conversations might be a year or two from now. Think about the significance they could have at home for the kids.

Consolidate your efforts. If you're able to get out to watch one of the kids in your ministry in something like a play or a sporting event, consider how you can use it as an opportunity to talk to parents as well. When I go to visit a student at a game, I often show up at the last thirty minutes, sit with the parents, and then go high-five the student at the end of the game. The parents think I'm awesome and as far as the student is concerned, I might as well have been there the entire time. Score!

Monitor your default. As a guy with a youth ministry background, it's easy for me to gravitate to students. It takes some intentionality for me to invest in relationships with parents and volunteers. Over the years, though, this tendency has become much easier to manage.

RECRUIT PARENTS TO COMMUNICATE FOR YOU

A number of years ago we experienced a tragedy that turned into an incredible work of God. I met a student in our youth ministry who had a passion for missions and serving, and would do anything to make others laugh. His humor and mischievousness was well known to all. Tragically, on a sunny Sunday evening in September, his life was cut short in a car accident while he was on his way to his girlfriend's youth group.

That week, in a packed auditorium full of families and countless high school students, his dad gave a wonderful message that stirred people to tears and laughter, sometimes both at the same time. What was so powerful that day was the way in which his dad depicted his love for missions and serving. I would never have predicted what would happen in the months to come as we planned a mission trip for the following summer. Not only had the youth ministry grown significantly in the midst of tragedy, but we also found ourselves planning a mission trip for a gigantic number of students as well as his mom, dad, and two sisters. God had indeed begun to show us how he can use a human tragedy to make an eternal difference.

As I sat down with my team, I wondered how we could possibly create a manageable way to raise funds for such a large number of people. Then there was the question of communication. How on earth could we communicate with so many families? It was a task of massive proportions that I'd never encountered before. We needed help. Specifically, we needed parents to help communicate the details and to get other parents and their kids to attend the mission trip meetings.

What happened is we pinpointed five or six parents who were well-established and known in our church. I asked them if they would be the ones to make phone calls, answer questions, and help plan the mission team meetings. To my surprise, they all said yes. They were so excited to support such an incredible move of God. All I needed to do was provide the contact information for all the families and the information for the trip. One solid informational meeting with my parent volunteers was multiplied as they reached out to parents in a personal way that communicated professionalism, care, and of course, good information! They made the calls, answered questions, and reminded parents about the times and dates for the meetings. And, wouldn't you know it, we had nearly 100 percent attendance at the missions meetings and a surplus of funds.

The fruit of recruiting parents to communicate with other parents is that they'll take ownership of the ministry with greater zeal and excitement. When that happens, they also become your best promoters.

Make Use of Social Media

I've been blogging and writing articles for well over a decade now, and I think I've adapted well to utilizing social media for my blog. I've also reaped the benefits of employing social media to communicate the vision and details of my ministries. I know this isn't the case for all of my fellow church workers. I have friends who tell me they don't have time to be following their friend's latest posts detailing what they had for breakfast. I understand where they're coming from, to a degree. At the same time, they're missing out on a valuable way to communicate with parents and their kids both the vision and details about their ministry. The fact is, social media is here to stay, and it's a mode of communication that the upcoming generations are flocking to. It's also a mode parents are flocking to if they're monitoring their kids' activity on the Internet. And, quite frankly, many parents are just as addicted to social media as their kids are.

So how can we make the most of social media in our ministries? Here are a few thoughts.

Only post what's helpful. One of the keys to keeping parents engaged is to ensure that your communication is helpful to them and is something they'll want to keep coming back to. Provide information that helps and supports parents, such as articles on parenting or social media, or insightful statistics on raising children. Also, comment in your posts about what you think is most helpful about the resources you share. A few words from you will make the communication stick with greater effectiveness. They become another way to pursue your vision of reaching and equipping the next generation by equipping parents. Remember, *they* are the heroes and you are there to guide them and support them on their journey. When you continue to see them in this light, you will find articles and resources that are helpful to *them*.

Create dialogue and create community. I spend quite a lot of time on social media. There's a plethora of quirky and funny pictures, great quotes to be inspired by, and even some articles by people in ministry. But for me, one of the best things about social media is that I get to engage with some great people who are in the trenches of ministry, just like I am. The problem is, there are many who just want to post their latest article in the hopes that I'll read it. They're not really interested in talking about what they've posted. While I'm always interested in reading articles and hearing new ideas, it's so much easier to engage with content from people who've taken the time to create a two-way dialogue. This is true for parents as well. While it's great to post information, articles, and resources, it's essential to ask questions and create conversations with the people you expect to read your posts.

In my experience, creating conversation on social media works best by asking simple questions that appeal to a wide range of people. If we are able to create social media groups for parents, not only do great questions allow us to build bridges with parents, it also allows them to build community with each other. Before you know it, they are sharing stories and helpful resources. Or, maybe more importantly, being vulnerable to reach out to share a parenting struggle. When you see this happening, you know you are on the right track. Here are some examples of things I've asked parents in the past:

- What is your family doing for the holidays?
- What family traditions do you have for Christmas?
- What are your favorite summer outings you've taken with your family?
- What's one thing you're doing to help your kids talk about God at home?
- What's one thing your kids love about kids' church or youth group?
- What advice would you give to a parent who's barely keeping up with a crazy schedule?

Respond to comments and questions. Conversation is a two-way street. As you consider how to engage with parents on social media, ensure that you're responding to their comments and questions and not just expecting them to respond to yours. An unanswered comment or post can be like ignoring a parent in the hallway at church. While it takes some time out of our schedules, posting a response is a valuable way of building rapport with the parents who entrust their kids to us each week.

Guard your time. Social media can take over your life if you're not careful. Maybe you've already learned that the hard way. For some it's not hard to waste away hours checking in on social media feeds and then suddenly realize they haven't gotten anything done. For those who would describe themselves as "social media inept," the wasted hours can go to just trying to figure out what they're doing. And then there are those for whom the idea of using social media seems like a great waste of time overall. In a world where more and more parents and their kids are using social media as their primary platform for communication, it's crucial that we get into their world and begin to communicate in the spaces they occupy. The great news is that, with a few simple steps, you can make social media work for you without getting either consumed or overwhelmed by it.

Consolidate your postings. I currently use a social media management tool that allows me to create posts that go out over numerous social networks at the same time. If you're going to use social media effectively—whether you're social media savvy or not—using this kind of tool is vital. It'll save you valuable time. I could give you the names of some of the tools I use, but chances are there's an even better one that's been developed since

I wrote this. The best way to find a good tool is to type "social media management tool" into the search field of your web browser. You'll find a long list of articles that give reviews on the latest and best ones to use.

Schedule in advance. If you're busy like me, it's often challenging to keep up with consistently posting information for parents to view. It's also a fact that the content you and I post will be in parents' feeds for a short amount of time, and then it won't show up again. A good social media management tool can help you deal with those things, too. It'll enable you to easily schedule the delivery of content throughout the week and only have to think about it once. A former youth pastor I used to lead would say that he wasn't the most social media-savvy guy around. Even though he's quite a bit younger than me, he never seemed to get into the world of social media (in some ways I am secretly jealous of people like him). However, he understood that his students and parents were spending a lot of time engaging with social media, and therefore it became an essential platform for him to utilize. That's why every Monday he scheduled his posts, texts, and emails to go out during the week. Apart from checking in to reply to questions or comments, he didn't have to think about posting for the rest of week.

Post pictures. It's great to communicate about programs and events, but there's nothing better than posting photos of kids having a blast in your ministry. If you want to keep parents coming back to your page, give them more than just information. Give them the smiles, laughter, and excitement found in the photos of their kids. Pictures can create engagement and excitement for your ministry. But, beware! Before posting pictures of kids, ensure that you have permission from parents. We include a place for them to grant their permission on all our registration and medical waiver forms.

I used to take it personally when parents didn't read my emails or know about an event I had painstakingly planned for them or their kids. I've met countless children's and youth ministry workers who've wondered if parents really care. Even worse, there have been times I've wondered if parents were simply choosing to ignore me. What I've found is that it all comes down to whether or not I'm communicating effectively. Whether I'm intentionally getting my message out with enough frequency and variety to break through the promotion dilution experienced by parents today. Whether I'm taking the time to get to know parents and their needs and preferences the way

I need to. If I'm getting those things right, I can be confident parents will receive the information they need for me to partner with them effectively.

Be Consistent. Whatever you plan to do for communication, ensure that you consider your sustainability to ensure consistency. As someone who blogs and posts on social media, I have constantly read the same advice from other bloggers: The key to engagement is consistent helpful content. Don't start too fast here, thinking sustainability and consistency first.

GAME SUMMARY

In a world of competing messages, it's imperative to communicate strategically, simply, and consistently.

PRACTICE DRILLS

1. Take 10 minutes to create a basic communication plan for your ministry. What are some things you can do to communicate on a weekly basis? Monthly? Yearly? In the next week, run your plan by two or three other team members, volunteers, or parents for their feedback. Then choose one item from your plan and begin to implement it.

2. Take a look at the social media networks you currently use. Search the Internet for articles and resources that could help you improve the way you use social media for your ministry. How could you use social media for communicating information about your ministry or upcoming events? What resources could you best provide the parents in your ministry by posting them on social media?

3. Create a small card to hand out to parents that they can complete in a minute or less. Include a place for them to write their name, email address, phone numbers, the social media they use, and their preferred modes of communication.

4. Evaluate how much of your time is given to investing relationally in parents. What can you do to improve the way you go about building relationships with parents? What's one thing you can do this week to build rapport with one of the parents in your ministry?

5. Create a list of responsibilities you typically have on a Sunday morning. Identify one or two of those responsibilities you could hand off to someone in order to make time for connecting with parents, and identify the people you could hand those things off to. Contact those people and begin planning for them to take over those responsibilities.

Endnotes

[1] http://www.businessinsider.com/how-many-contacts-does-it-take-before-someone-buys-your-product-2011-7.

[2] https://mailchimp.com/resources/email-marketing-benchmarks/. Accessed August 12, 2020.

[3] https://www.ftc.gov/tips-advice/business-center/guidance/can-spam-act-compliance-guide-business. Accessed August 16, 2020.

Chapter 6

PROVIDE RESOURCES

BE AN EXPERT AT HELPING PARENTS FIND ANSWERS, RATHER THAN ONE WHO'S EXPECTED TO HAVE THE ANSWERS.

"**H**ow can I talk to my kids about sex?" That was the question (or something like it) one of my best volunteers asked me a number of years ago. To be honest, I still can't recall his exact words, simply because I was so stunned that he'd even asked. You see, at the time, I looked up to him as a wise and God-honoring man who seemed to have life figured out. I didn't have any kids at the time, and the idea of having kids myself was a little intimidating. It wouldn't be long before I'd be asking him how to survive the early, sleepless years of being a new parent. So, why would he ask me such a heavy question that I felt so unqualified to answer? As I reflected on this and many similar questions over the years, I've learned an extremely valuable lesson that's improved the way I minister to parents ever since. No matter how inadequate I may feel, parents see me as the "go to" expert in matters involving their kids. The same is true for you.

You're the expert whether you know it or not. It doesn't matter if you're a volunteer or paid staff. It doesn't matter if you're single or married, or whether you have kids or not. The fact that you've chosen to be active in the field of children's, youth, or family ministry automatically qualifies you in the eyes of parents. I know there'll be some parents who'll always see you as the baby-sitter to their kids, but there's a greater number of parents who'll look to you for answers and expertise. You might not be an expert in parenting, but you're well on your way to becoming an expert on kids, or at least that's how parents will view you if you stick around for a while.

It's nice to have others see us as the experts. But what happens when the rubber meets the road? What happens when parents really need an answer from you, and you simply have no idea? The good news is that being an expert doesn't mean that parents really expect you to have all the answers, but they're hoping you can help them to find good answers. On top of that, most parents understand you're busy and there may be too much content to cover in the time you have available. There have been many times a parent has made the assumption I'm busy with their kids and have little time for them. Not long ago, a parent said to me, "I know you're busy. Can you point me to something that will help me understand technology better? My kids are online more and more, and I want to keep them safe." By pointing parents to resources, you're actually able to give them relatively short answers while still giving them the information they need.

BECOME A STUDENT OF RESOURCES

As someone who works with children and students, you'll naturally have greater access to resources than many of your parents will ever be aware of. It's imperative that you and I become eyes and ears for parents regarding what's available to them. Let's look at some different ways you can build a list of resources to suggest to parents.

Ask your peers. The other children's and youth ministry workers you know have experience you can draw from, both in ministry and as parents themselves. Chances are they know of books, websites, and articles that are helpful for parents. When I was creating content for a parent workshop, I sent about ten messages to friends of mine who are also in ministry and asked them to tell me what they considered to be the best resources for the topic that the workshop was on. Within a day or so, I had some solid resources that I was able to start reviewing and using. The great news is that a number of them referred me to the same resources, essentially giving me a solid endorsement. Being able to stand in front of parents and tell them that a number of credible sources recommended a particular resource goes a long way when we don't have time to check out every resource ourselves.

Consult parents. There are parents in your ministry who are utilizing some great resources you don't know anything about. In a previous church, I met one mom who just loved to read and was fully invested in her kid's faith journey. Over time, I was able to recommend a number of resources she had read and gained some great insights from. In fact, with her permission, I was able to refer parents to her for certain questions she had investigated for herself. In some sense, she became the parenting expert other parents looked to for advice and resources. If you don't know who the parents like this are in your ministry, start asking parents what books or websites have been most helpful to them in their parenting and why. If you have a social media page, you could post the question there. If not, find ways to weave it into conversations with parents you're getting to know.

Seek out professionals. Identify the professionals in your church or community who are trusted to help families. Include those who are highly regarded by others, such as Christian counselors, marriage and family therapists, and pediatricians. These are the people who'll have the best answers for the families you minister to. Your role is simply to refer parents to them. If you don't know who those people are, talk to the people in your church who've been around a while and can help you pinpoint good experts in the field of marriage and family. I met "Dee Dee" when I arrived in a new role overseeing Family Ministry. Not only had she lived in the community for decades, she also was the overseer of the care ministry for the church. She had been in that role well over 20 years. Not only did she know people in the community, but she automatically had a good understanding of which professionals would be the best fit for a given family. It's so helpful having someone who knows the reputation and regard of counselors and doctors in the area. Who is your Dee Dee?

Create a resource file. Over time, I've found it helpful to build up a file of resources and contacts for parents. There's no way in the world that I can remember all the books, websites, or people that would be helpful to recommend. Having a resource file gives me a place to keep all that information at my fingertips. One of my ongoing goals is to have parents oversee a resource file and become the one who seeks out great resources to refer to parents. Not everyone wants to work directly with kids and students and would prefer to be behind the scenes. Who are those parents at your church? Whether you have such a parent in your ministry or not, keeping a file of resources is still crucial.

Have parents review resources. Parents listen to parents. One of the most effective ways to provide helpful resources is to get a parent to read a book or to use a resource and then review it. Whether it's posted on social media, the church website, or in printed form, parents are more likely to utilize a resource that's endorsed by another parent. Find a great resource, have a parent review it, share it on social media, and get parents to comment to win the resource!

How to Write a Resource Review

As you consider asking parents to review resources, here are some guidelines to help them know what to look for.

- Keep the review under 400 words.
- Who is the resource best suited for?
- Why is this resource helpful for parents to read/use?
- What about this resource was most helpful to you as a parent?
- Where can parents buy this resource? How much does it cost?

Become a Giver of Resources

So often the time that's afforded us on a Sunday morning or during a midweek program is limited in terms of what we can say to parents. When parents come to me with a question, there's a tendency in me to want to answer their question and bring complete closure to the issue they're facing. But to provide adequate help to parents in a few minutes is unrealistic. Referring parents to a good resource is a better way to go, especially if you really don't have good knowledge on a particular subject or issue.

In addition to the resources you might be able to mention to parents off the cuff in a conversation, there are other ways you can make various resources readily available to parents.

Create a resource stand. At the entrances to your ministry environments, create a resource hub right at the check-in area. Stock it with a number of books you recommend, your latest ministry brochure, calendar information, and parent take-home sheets for that week's kids' and students' messages. Having the stand in your check-in area allows parents to see helpful resources and calendar information every week when they drop their kids off. For a digital alternative, create a virtual resource parent hub on your church's website, and consider creating a postcard at check-in that promotes and points them to your online resource parent hub.

Provide a weekly take-home/parent page. A variety of curricula provide a take-home resource for parents that allow them to engage in the content with their kids throughout the week. If you don't have a resource like this, consider making it a part of your lesson creation each week. Being able to provide parents with a bottom line from the lesson, the Bible verses used, and some questions they can ask their kids is a great start. But keep in mind the possibility that a take-home sheet might not even make it home. It might get left at church or could end up in the monthly trash pile that gathers in the family's minivan. Consider other ways to get it into parents' hands or find creative ways to bring it to the focus of parents. You could send it as part of a weekly email or post it on the church website. Once it's home, we've found that making it into a monthly laminated dinner placemat is a great way to make discussion questions part of family mealtimes.

Have kids give their parents "homework." This is one of the best ideas I've heard recently. What kid wouldn't want to give their parents an assignment to complete? Whether it's interacting with the take-home/parent page or reading an article, recruiting kids to assign something for their parents to do is a great way to resource parents.

Because I've been around a long time, there are many occasions when a parent will ask a question to which I know the answer. However, it's crucial that I see my role as an equipper of parents rather than as someone who's quick to provide solutions. Having more experience can actually become a barrier to helping equip parents since we will often give an answer we have read, rather than helping a parent find the answer. If I'm able to point them to a good book or article that gets them to dig deeper into an issue or question, it's far better than a quick answer in the hallway at church. It increases the likelihood that they'll own the information and answers they find. You never know, they might even become good candidates for providing reviews and recommendations of resources for others.

GAME SUMMARY

By resourcing parents, you move from having to know all the answers to helping parents find the answers for themselves.

PRACTICE DRILLS

1. Ask parents to identify their "go-to" websites for parenting help. Post the question on social media to increase your range of answers. Use the responses to create a list you can share with other parents. (You may want to do a brief check of the websites you include on the list—or have a trusted parent check them out—to make sure they're appropriate.)

2. Ask parents in your ministry to tell you what their felt needs are when it comes to the kind of resources they're looking for. Use their responses to guide you in your search for resources. Make a goal of finding at least two or three resources for each for the felt needs the parents identified.

3. If you have children, create a list of books, podcasts, or curricula you have benefitted from and you could share with parents. Make that list available on a resource stand, the church website, or via social media.

4. With their permission, publish a list of "experts" in your church who can be a resource for parents, including counselors, physicians, educators, and "been there" parents. Include a notice to parents that just because these individuals are part of the church does not mean their services are free (unless otherwise noted), and that appropriate compensation may be expected at the time of service.

5. Assemble a parent resource team to help you brainstorm different ways to provide resources for parents and creative ways to help parents continue spiritual conversations with their children at home.

Chapter 7

EQUIP DISENGAGED PARENTS

HOW TO TRAIN AND EQUIP PARENTS WHEN THEY WON'T EVEN SHOW UP.

There are times when I feel like being in ministry set me up with unrealistic expectations for raising kids of my own. Teaching someone else's kids is a piece of cake compared to teaching my own kids the simplest of things. When it's someone else's kids, it's easier to switch off, head home, and move on emotionally. Even when I've had a bad day in ministry and have had to deal with "that kid," I can still sleep relatively easy at night.

Having my own kids is a totally different ball game. Being a dad has given me more gray hairs and has resulted in less hair overall. Some people call gray hair "a crown of wisdom." I call it a significant battle scar. My kids say I'm just getting old. I say they're the reason my crown is getting so thin. But I wouldn't change it for the world.

Being a parent is the most frustrating, rewarding, challenging, interesting, and joyous role I've ever entered into. I'm so thankful for the many voices that have come alongside me as I've often bumbled my way through being a husband and father. In particular, I'm forever thankful to my friend and mentor Ron. Ron has been in ministry for 45 years or more (and is still going strong, he would add). I'm thankful for the wisdom and resources he's passed along to help me on my journey in marriage, parenting, and ministry. I know a lot about the latest resources that can help me in my own pursuit of being a good parent. But there's nothing quite like Ron coming alongside me to give me insights, tools, and the face-to-face encouragement that I really can do it.

All parents need someone to help and encourage them as they navigate through the journey of raising their kids. It's one thing to have resources. It's quite another thing to be equipped by people who are invested in you and your family. But if you don't have someone in your life to help equip you for marriage and family, you're in good company. That's the reality for many, if not most, parents.

OVERCOMING THE OBSTACLES

Equipping and resourcing are vastly different things when it comes to partnering with parents. To state it simply, resourcing parents is focused on pointing parents to materials or helps they can utilize for themselves. Equipping parents involves developing their knowledge and skills by teaching, training, and encouraging them. Every parent in your ministry needs greater equipping and support, and you might be the best person to help them.

When I was in my early years of ministry, the idea of equipping parents wouldn't have been on my radar. If someone came along and wrote a book like this and attempted to convince me to provide parent training or seminars, I'd have skipped to the next chapter citing that I was too young and inexperienced to do such a thing.

If you're a veteran reading this, you might have already attempted some kind of seminar and given up following a low turnout that consisted of the parents who already "get it." A friend who was also in children's ministry had this to say to me a number of years ago:

> Parent meetings and parent seminars are a waste of time! No one shows up to them and even if you can get parents to show up, they're usually the ones who are already making an attempt to do the right things. What about all the parents who don't know or don't care? How can I help them?

Quite frankly, I had to agree with him. In my experience, it had always been challenging to get parents to show up to an informational meeting, and even more challenging to get them to show up for a parent seminar. Since my conversation with my friend, parents—in my opinion—have only become more stressed and overscheduled. Why would they ever be interested in a training seminar?

While I'd all but given up trying to get parents to show up for meetings and seminars, my pushback to my friend was,

> But there's got to be a way to engage parents and give them the tools they need to raise their kids. It's too important to simply give up. They're with their kids so much more than us. They have greater influence and impact on their kids! We've got to find a way in!

I'd previously had many other conversations that were pushing me toward approaching the issue differently. But this was the conversation that made me say, "That's it! I've got to do this!"

I later had my opportunity. I was a new guy in a completely new role. My new church had never had a "Family Ministry Pastor" before. As a church, they had some incredible ministry environments from birth through high school, and a wonderfully innovative family ministry team, which I was now charged to lead. As a whole, the children's and youth ministries were working as a cohesive team. My role would be to lead the team to greater cohesion, help rebuild a struggling youth ministry, and—here's the exciting part—develop and implement a strategic plan to partner with parents.

I essentially had a blank canvas and a great deal of freedom and trust. If there was ever a time to try something new or tweak something old, it had come. This British Bulldog was determined to reach and equip parents to raise their kids with a solid faith foundation through an experiment called "ParentWise." Motivated by my prior experience with poorly attended parent meetings and my friend's comments about such meetings being a waste of time, I began pursuing the goal of creating a series of seminars for three groups of parents: parents of children birth through kindergarten, parents of elementary-aged children, and parents of middle school and high school students.

When I first started to dream up ParentWise, I kept referring to it as an "experiment" as a way to cover my bases just in case it failed. (If you ever hear a leader refer to a new ministry or program as an "experiment," you can be quite sure that leader has no idea how it's really going to turn out.) But to call ParentWise an "experiment" might suggest that I jumped in without having a plan or purpose. But that was far from the truth. Since the conversation about the value of parent meetings with my friend, I'd given a great deal of thought about how best to reach and equip parents. I was especially driven by one crucial question: How could I reach those parents who hadn't traditionally shown up for meetings and seminars?

LESSONS TO LEARN FROM

I always thought there was a magic bullet to reaching parents; that I'd go to a conference and discover some innovative idea for it that would solve all my problems. Sometimes, when things aren't working in ministry, there's this tendency to gravitate to the latest thing or implement something that worked in a church somewhere else without considering how it will work in our own contexts. Consequently, there's also a tendency to overlook simple answers that were there all along. But the truth is, much of what I've discovered—and am still discovering—really isn't rocket science. Simply put, what my team achieved through ParentWise was largely built around common sense and a willingness to evaluate and adapt. As an aside, when we go to conferences and hear about incredible ministry programs, we must fully realize these great programs had to start somewhere. There was an idea, a plan, and a willingness to make some mistakes, fail a little, succeed a little, and evaluate and adapt. Don't compare your early efforts with a tried and tested program you hear about.

I used to think that parent seminars were outdated and the goal of reaching and equipping parents was unreachable. Our experience with ParentWise changed that perspective. Attendance was much better than I had ever experienced, and the feedback we got from parents was not only positive, it included requests to cover other areas of parenting as well. We also saw parents join small groups with other parents they had connected with at ParentWise. That wasn't something we had planned. It just happened. And it makes me wonder what would've been the outcome if we had planned that next step for parents better.

With those things in mind, what follows are some of the key lessons I learned about equipping parents from developing and implementing ParentWise. If you grab onto them, they'll offer you the ability to reach and equip parents in ways that can be implemented wherever you are.

Listen to parents. Equipping isn't primarily about you or me; it's about parents. I'm sure we both know that, but so often what we attempt to provide parents is more about us and our agenda for them than it is about their genuine needs and concerns. From the perfectly planned presentation for getting parents to buy into our ministries to the parent workshop focused on making church a greater priority, we can tend to be motivated by what's in it for us.

Now, there's nothing inherently wrong with those kinds of meetings. Sometimes they're necessary. But they're not going to draw a crowd. And let's be honest, the parents who do show up at those meetings usually show up for everything you do, anyway. With that in mind, what does it take to get parents intrigued enough to give time to show up at a meeting or seminar? What I've discovered is that they'll give their time when we take time to invest in their felt needs.

Just take a moment to think about the parents in your ministry. What are their greatest needs? What are their greatest struggles as parents? What do they wish someone would tell them?

Now, maybe I'm just a little slow on the uptake, but for so many years I had looked for ideas to engage parents with information and support in ways that I thought would be helpful. However, it never occurred to me to ask them what would be most helpful. Maybe as a younger leader I was afraid to ask, or maybe I thought I knew what they needed. Either way, in my busyness I never slowed down enough to consider what parents really needed from me. Perhaps deep down inside I didn't consider I could actually help parents (especially in my early years when I was single and didn't have kids). However, as I took time to sit down and talk with parents, I discovered an essential key to partnering with them: listening. So much of ministry emphasizes how you and I speak and communicate. Yet, listening well to parents is the first step on the path to partnering with them. That's because listening builds bridges of trust.

Until I had my own kids, I never understood the feelings of insecurity most parents feel from day to day. Most parents I meet are all too aware of their own flaws and those of their kids. Many of them live in the unrealistic hopes that you and I will never discover the real family that lives behind the "forced church smile." I know this feeling all too well.

It was a Sunday morning, and we were running late. Our youngest had food all over his face, our oldest had changed her outfit at least three times, and our middle child was determined to do the opposite of whatever Lisa or I asked. (Don't you just love middle children?) The instructions to hurry up were no longer polite requests; rather they turned into blood curdling tirades that were likely being heard by parts of our neighborhood. We jumped into a minivan that's a perfect representation of our lives—it looks like someone stocked it full of diapers, toys, candy wrappers, and old socks, then threw in a hand grenade. As we drove a mile to church, the chaos continued as the kids bickered and whined, Lisa and I dissected who's to blame for being late—yet again. We arrived at church, the van doors opened, and immediately we all jumped into church mode and the forced Sunday smiles appeared again. What would happen if people really found out about my imperfect family?

I've come to realize that I can't really hide my family flaws, and it doesn't help others be honest about their struggles when I try. There are parents all over our churches who are attempting to hide their family flaws and keep up appearances while feeling absolutely isolated and alone. That's why it's imperative that you and I live with openness about our own challenges. It helps them realize we're flawed too. We also need to take time to listen to parents' real concerns and discover the real people behind the facades. When we open up our lives to parents and take time to listen to them, we're helping them be real as well, and ultimately building bridges of trust between us and them.

Someone once said, "Speak in such a way that others love to listen to you. Listen in such a way that others love to speak to you." By leaning in and listening to what's important to parents, we also begin to gain vital insights into their most pressing concerns. And those insights are what enable us to create meetings and seminars parents will want to give their time to because they know they'll receive content they need to hear.

Address parents' present concerns. Most parents are living in survival mode and want answers for the most pressing issues of the day. We need to create seminars and meetings for parents centered on those issues. When we listen, learn, and understand our parents, we create solutions they really need. Once, I did a parent workshop called, "Parenting in Survival Mode," for parents of elementary-age kids. For families with kids at that age, schedules are starting to pick up the pace, and there seems to be a never-ending list of activities (and expenses) for parents. Parents in this season of life feel like they're barely treading water most of the time, and survival has very possibly taken the place of passing on faith to their kids. They're looking for someone to help them slow down, take a deep breath, and focus. With a captive audience, this was a great opportunity to cast a Deuteronomy 6:4-9 vision and give some simple and practical steps for utilizing teachable times and creating intentional moments without adding to an already maxed out schedule.

Create a parent team. It's always easier to do things myself. It can get messy when others are involved. And involving parents, in particular, can take things to a whole new level of messiness. So why would I want to recruit parents to help me? One word: ownership. When parents are involved, they take on a vested interest in seeing the activities they're a part of succeed. When that happens, parents also become natural promoters of those activities, increasing the potential reach of those things. That's true whether the activities are events and programs for kids or parent seminars. Greater ownership produces greater results. When what we're doing is simply "our thing," parents won't make as much of an investment. But when it's "their thing," they'll be inclined to make a greater effort and help others to do the same.

The other benefit that comes with involving parents in what you do is the ability to delegate. While delegating requires some added communication on your part, it also frees you up to focus on assembling and delivering the content at a meeting without being consumed with the nuts and bolts of planning and implementation as well. As you recruit parents to help you put on meetings and seminars, be thinking about people who can help you promote the event, greet participants and help them get registered, serve refreshments, provide childcare, and even present content. By getting people plugged into just those simple, strategic roles, you've lightened your load and increased the number of people committed to seeing the meeting succeed.

Utilize parents and other experts. One of the struggles I've faced in considering how to equip parents is feeling like I have to know it all. I'll never have enough time or experience to equip parents in every area in which they need help. That's a reality for all of us in ministry. The great news is that you and I don't have to know it all. In fact, I've discovered it's actually to my advantage to have experts and peers create and deliver content rather than trying to do it all myself. I'm not talking about paying a speaker thousands of dollars to come in and speak to parents. I'm talking about involving people who are in your community and in your church. Let me give you a couple of examples.

I once provided two workshops to parents of middle school and high school students based specifically on their felt needs. We surveyed parents, and the clear message we got was they needed help protecting their kids in regard to technology and drugs. Not too long before, some students in the community had been in trouble for "sexting," and a recent graduate had died from a heroin overdose. Many parents were overwhelmed with fear and concern for their kids as a result. I knew I had to do something to address those concerns. But here was the problem: I didn't have time to create content, and I certainly didn't have the expertise to provide anything of significance to my parents. As I talked with some key parents and staff at my church, we were able to pinpoint some people and organizations in the area that had expertise in these areas of need.

After a number of phone calls and "getting to know you" meetings (don't miss this step), I was able to recruit a local school drug counselor, a drug task force detective, and a police detective who was an expert in technology. All I really had to do was give them a good picture of what I was looking for, a sense of what to expect from our parents, and some guidelines for time and how the workshop would run. And here's the best part: they were free. What I discovered as I made phone calls to the local schools, police departments, and counselors is that it's in their interests to get out into the community. It was also essential to talk to my church leadership and ensure they were in support of the speakers I was looking to bring in. For me, that was no problem. In fact, when the drug task force detective asked permission to bring "samples" of drugs into the workshop, my executive director fully supported the idea. Now, just in case you are wondering what I mean by "samples" let me be clear. The samples were purely for parents to look at in order for them to understand what drugs look like and how they're packaged.

Perhaps the most startling thing about utilizing experts is how they can become a great promotional draw. While I like to think that parents love the quirky English guy, they'd rather hear from an expert on a drug task force or an expert in technology. What's more, given that we weren't providing any Christian content in the workshops, the local school system actually provided promotion for us through the newsletters and regular emails. Both workshops were very well attended and we had a large number of people from our community who had never been to our church or any church at all. How about that? The drug counselor shared that this was the largest group of parents he'd ever spoken to and loved how invested our church was. It was also a great bridge builder with the school system. It opened up the opportunity for me to be part of an advisory committee and panel of presenters for a parent workshop they were holding on bullying. How about that? I had a plan, but God had a bigger plan.

An example of someone in my church who was able to present content to parents is Mike. I met Mike quite early on at a church in Michigan. At the time, he was a parent to teenagers and a great guy with an incredibly positive attitude that's just infectious. He's also a great husband and father. Everything I've observed about him and the way he lives out his faith is absolutely authentic. What's more is that others hold him in high regard and look to him as a leader in our church. That's one of the reasons why I sought him out to grab a coffee a couple of years ago. As we talked faith, family, and his work, we got back to the subject that most people ask me about. "How is ministry going for you?" That particular week I was in the beginning stages of creating content for a workshop called "Parenting for Purity." As we talked, Mike shared some steps he had taken with each of his sons that had become defining milestones in their faith journeys and had also helped them understand God's plan for sexuality. It suddenly hit me that other parents needed to hear Mike's story. So, a month later, I interviewed Mike as he shared some practical and specific steps he used to talk to his kids about sex.

There's a twofold lesson I learned from having Mike share. First, since Mike is in the trenches of parenting teenagers, his story held more weight than anything I could have shared. Second, there are a lot more "Mikes" in our church who've navigated through certain seasons of raising kids and have come out the other side with wisdom and hope to offer. One such parent was Trish. She came to me and expressed her heart to partner with parents and pass on what she'd learned on her parenting journey so far. (When people keep hearing the vision from you and me, they'll come and seek us out when it captures their heart.) Trish quickly became someone who helped me equip and train parents from birth through elementary age.

You and I can't be experts in everything, but there are people in your community and church who can lend their expertise and experience to providing great content that'll help equip parents. They'll also likely draw greater numbers than you or I can.

Schedule strategically. One of the biggest reasons parent workshops fail is poor scheduling. It's not because they aren't valuable or important. A number of years ago, I attended a friend's church that had flown in a nationally acclaimed speaker for a parenting seminar. While it was a great parenting seminar, I was somewhat shocked that more parents didn't show up for those few hours on a Saturday morning. In trying to think of what kept people from being there, Saturday morning kids sports, weekend projects, and family time were just a few of the conflicts I could come up with. And while those things didn't seem like significant conflicts to me, they were significant in the community where my friend ministered.

One of the reasons parents don't attend parenting workshops is simply because they don't have margin to add another thing into their schedules. In between work, their kid's schedules, and their typical family rhythms, it's hard to expect them to show up on another evening of the week—or perhaps their only free evening of the week—to be a family together. Therefore, it's imperative to schedule times of equipping when they're naturally and normally on campus at our churches. Parents of young kids find it difficult to show up to a midweek parent workshop because mealtimes and bedtimes are a limiting factor. Parents of middle school and high school students barely have another night of the week available as they're living in "taxi driver" mode during the week. So, the question we have to ask ourselves is, "Given our church schedules, when are these two parent groups naturally and normally at church?" And the answer to that question has to drive the way in which we schedule events for parents.

For many churches, parents of younger children are around on Sunday mornings, so that's often the best time to provide a parent workshop. For middle school and high school there's often midweek programs, and many parents use this time to go grocery shopping or get laundry done while their kids are busy, for many others it's an open evening since they have to come to the church to drop off and pick up their kids, anyway. In the past, I've provided workshops on Wednesday evenings that were well attended and well received since they didn't require parents to drastically change their schedules.

Provide community, not just content. One of the greatest ways you and I can support parents is to help them get connected with each other. Many parents feel as though they have to keep up appearances. Consequently, they also feel alone and think that other parents are getting it right while they're getting it all wrong. It's not until they get to sit around a table and talk to other parents that they realize they're not alone and there are many other parents who feel just as messed up as they do. That's why it's essential to create opportunities in workshops for parents to talk with each other about the content. It not only helps them apply what they're hearing; it enables them to connect with and build community with other parents as well. I've seen friendships and supportive relationships begin at a workshop and continue after it's over and done.

Give options. No matter what you do, there will never be a good way to reach everyone and get every parent to a workshop. When Covid-19 became a new reality for all of us, we all had to quickly change how we operated. While video training does not provide the in-person personal touch and community building opportunities, I think we are learning there are ways in which we can deliver good content. And perhaps now people are more open to some of these delivery methods too?

Another option is to consider offering video modules. We've seen greater development of online "Master Classes" as companies and organizations create training classes people subscribe to online. Essentially, they are prerecorded video classes with an outline to follow along with, some next steps, and coaching questions. Again, you might lose some ability to build community that way, but it's better than a parent missing the content entirely.

Keep in mind that not all of these options will work well for you in your context. It might be a case of trying options and using your parent network to gain feedback on what works best. Even better, there might be a parent who could become a part of your team to help set up the video training elements for you. It's also possible that you aren't at a point of being able to create workshops yet. Don't worry, that used to be me. However, consider some of the small steps you can take to equip parents in being the primary investors in their child's faith journey:

- Refer parents to books and videos that could be helpful to them.
- Encourage parents to get involved in small groups or classes that are designed to equip parents.
- Seek out empty nesters or veteran parents who could serve as mentors to parents who are looking for help.
- Promote parent workshops at other churches in your area.

Every parent needs help somewhere along the way. We can provide them that help by equipping them for the journey. When we schedule strategically, provide content that meets parents' felt needs, and involve others in the process, we can create opportunities for equipping parents that they'll want to be a part of.

GAME SUMMARY

The biggest hurdle to equipping parents is getting them to show up, and to clear that hurdle we have to put their needs—not ours—first.

PRACTICE DRILLS

1. Create a survey to learn about the felt needs of the parents in your church. Ask questions about the kinds of topics they would like to learn about or struggles they could use help with the most. Based on the survey results, create a training seminar or workshop to address the most frequently mentioned felt needs.

2. Take a look at your typical church schedule and brainstorm with some of the parents in your ministry times that would be good for providing a parent seminar or workshop. Consider when parents are naturally and normally coming to your church. Then pencil a workshop into your calendar and begin planning for it.

3. Create a list of experts and parent peers in your community and church who could lead or teach in a workshop. Begin contacting those people to discuss the possibility of working with them to put on a parent equipping event.

4. Create a list of roles parents could fill that would enable them to take ownership of a parent equipping event. Then identify the key parents in your ministry who could fill those roles. Contact those parents and ask them to prayerfully consider participating.

5. If creating a series of workshops isn't an option for you right now, identify one thing you could do to help equip the parents in your ministry and begin doing it.

6. Identify opportunities in your community or through other churches or organizations for parents to receive training and promote them in your church's bulletin, website, or social media network.

Chapter 8

HAVE AN INTENTIONAL MINISTRY STRATEGY

HOW A CLEAR STRATEGY FOR MINISTRY HELPS YOU TO PARTNER WITH PARENTS.

I used to think that being a nice guy with a cool British accent was all I needed in ministry. That I would just have to open my mouth and word would get out about the guy with the great accent. That I could just throw out a few typically British phrases, people would trust me, and I could get parents to say "yes" to anything. After all, doesn't having an English accent make me trustworthy?

The answer to that is, "No." Relying on something like an accent is just shallow. In fact, when I get free stuff because of my accent, my wife reminds me of how shallow it really is. Shallow, yes. But who doesn't like to get free stuff?

Being a really nice person isn't a bad thing. And I'm told that having an accent makes me sound more intelligent. But parents (and their kids) need more than nice people and British accents to reach the next generation for Christ. It's likely you have a gift or a skill that has help you succeed in ministry, but parents do need more. They need a compelling vision and—more importantly—a strategy that can make that vision a reality.

The most successful churches I have seen always have well-crafted vision statements that would communicate what they saw as a hoped-for future. I've seen church leaders ask the staff and congregation to commit to and even to memorize those statements. (That wasn't for me, by the way. Bible memorization is enough of a challenge for me. Don't make me memorize statements as well.)

In addition to vision statements, churches have also added catchy taglines that capture people's attention and quickly communicate a church's most important values. Such taglines often strive to let visitors know what to expect from the church, as well as paint a clear picture of where the church is going.

As great as vision statements and taglines are, what gives them their power is having a strategy that enables you to live them out. Strategy is what tells you the steps you must take to move intentionally toward your hoped-for future or to put your most important values into practice. Vision statements and taglines only buy you time as you work toward seeing them become reality. People need to see constant movement toward the vision and to be reminded that each step moves them strategically closer to it.

There are plenty of things that happen by accident. But the greatest things happen when we take a God-given vision and prayerfully consider how to act on it. That's what this chapter is all about.

EFFECTIVE STRATEGIES BUILD CONFIDENCE AND TRUST

If a compelling biblical vision serves to capture the hearts of families in our churches, then a healthy strategy is what builds trust and confidence as parents and kids see that vision at work. Parents won't continue to send their kids to you just because people tell them you're really nice. Parents want to know the why and how of your ministry, too. When they see a plan that's in place and a strategy that's working, they're more likely to take you seriously.

Strategy also opens the door for parents to take greater ownership of reaching and equipping their kids for Christ. Once parents get involved in your ministry and see its inner workings, having a healthy strategy they can get behind will encourage them to get even more involved and invest in the lives of their kids. Haphazardness can hinder parents' willingness to partner with you. But having a clear strategy can open the doorway to parents letting you come alongside them to help them invest in their child's faith journey.

Depending on your ministry culture and your community, it's likely certain strategies will be more effective than others. What works in one context might not work at all in your context. However, when it comes to partnering with parents in reaching and equipping the next generation for Christ, there are some strategies that I believe are universal. Those strategies are what we'll look at in this chapter. But before we jump into some specific strategies to consider, let's look at *how* to implement your strategies in a sustainable and successful manner. In the book, *The Work of Leaders*, the authors point to a framework that provides a good balance of clear vision, alignment, and execution.[1] To implement a successful strategy, we will need to carefully consider how to communicate the "why" behind the strategy (vision), build alignment with key players, and ensure there's a clear plan for execution.

HAVE A SYNCHRONIZED TEAM APPROACH

Let's take a moment to revisit the rowing illustration from the beginning of Chapter 1. I mentioned there how important it is for a rowing team to be synchronized and row in the same direction. It's so important, in fact, that there's this little guy at the back of the boat whose primary responsibilities are to steer the boat and keep the team in sync. He's called the "Coxwain," or the "Cox." I used to think he was just a bossy boots who was there to tell the others to row faster. As a kid, I used to imagine he had a button that would give each rower an electric shock if they weren't going fast enough. However, it turns out that what he's really doing is coordinating the power and rhythm of the rowers by giving them clear instructions and keeping them motivated.[2] At the end of the race, the big burley rowers on the winning team grab this little guy and throw him so he goes high up into the air and then down into the murky brown River Thames. (That was always my favorite part.)

If rowing is an analogy for the local church, many of us find ourselves in a boat with a group of rowers who are out of sync with one another. As a result, we find ourselves going around in circles rather than moving forward. We paddle furiously in opposite directions, not even trying to coordinate our efforts. We see this most in the "silo" mentality that exists between our children's and youth ministries. They end up being either in competition with one another or so isolated from each other that there's no sense of continuity when children graduate from the children's ministry into the youth ministry. When it comes to reaching and equipping the next generation, there's no room for silos.

You probably have some good people on your team who have their oars in the water and are working hard toward a common vision. And, you probably have some people who are paddling furiously in other directions, making it hard for you to get anywhere. You also may have some people who've given up paddling altogether and feel like they're aimlessly floating along, wondering where you all are heading. Unfortunately, that third perspective can carry over and affect the confidence of the parents and kids in your ministry as well. When the people we lead begin to wonder what's going on, they can start to wander off; sometimes going to another church that seems to have a better plan, sometimes in the direction of unhealthy choices or behaviors, and sometimes wandering away from the church altogether. That's why it's imperative we commit to being part of a synchronized team that's rowing in the same direction.

Let's take a look at what that means in practical terms.

Begin with yourself. It just seems easier to work in a silo. When we knock the ball out of the park in our ministry areas, everyone's happy and we get the credit. When things go bad and no one has come out of their silos to help, we've got somewhere to place the blame (other than ourselves). But taking all the credit is just selfish, and placing the blame on others rather than owning it ourselves is a sign of weak leadership. The fact is, keeping synchronized with the rest of the team begins and ends with us. God has called us to be a part of the body of Christ—to work toward the common goal of reaching and equipping the next generation for Christ. We can't cut ourselves off from the rest of the body. It's essential that we invest ourselves in helping the body function in unity. If that means building bridges with other ministry areas or leaders, it's our responsibility to initiate those steps. We can't wait on them. There's too much at stake.

Get everyone in the same room. Synchronized teams don't just happen by accident. They begin with people like you and me taking the initiative to get in the same room as other key players. In my current ministry, we have a monthly family ministry meeting that consists of the children's and youth ministry staffs. The meeting is focused on training, sharing pertinent information, and discussing upcoming events. As for getting in the same room, we have little choice since we all share one office together. There are times that causes my ADD to get the better of me, but for the most part, it's a huge advantage having our team consistently working in the same physical space. You might not be part of team like ours or even have an office, but that doesn't mean you can't find ways to get in the same room as your team members from time to time. It might mean hosting a team meeting in your home, getting together at a coffee shop, or meeting up at a park. With a little creativity, the options are endless.

Coordinate your calendars. There's nothing worse than one ministry area struggling because another ministry in your church scheduled a big event on the same date. Not only is it frustrating for leaders and volunteers who've poured their hearts and souls into an event or program, but it's also frustrating for a family who has to pick one event over another. In my church, I have to ensure that I run every program and event through the keeper of the main church calendar first. Then I can coordinate with the children's and youth ministries. Sometimes, that requires me to move an event for the betterment of the whole team. But, that's what being a team player is all about. I tend to plan way in advance, but I realize there are team members who aren't always inclined the same way. I can't just say, "I got the date first, so deal with it!" On the other hand, neither can I always be changing events at the last minute because someone else didn't plan well. That's where getting in the same room on a regular basis truly helps. It forces me to ask questions of my team, consider their schedules, and evaluate how my schedule might help or hinder theirs.

Provide training and resources. A yearly training for your family ministry volunteers all in the same room is a good way to ensure they hear a unified vision and strategy. While there's some training that's only relevant to volunteers working with certain age groups or ministry areas, there are other things that you will want all of our family ministry volunteers to be exposed to, regardless of the age they work with. That includes things like our vision, a unified strategy, safety procedures, how to partner with parents, and any special emphasis you want all volunteers to hear. Utilizing the same training and resources in a large group format for these kinds of topics is far more efficient and cost effective. It also ensures the approach to those issues is common throughout all the age groups.

A successful format I have used for these yearly training meetings is to have a large group session where, for about 5-10 minutes apiece, we cover the three or four key topics we want everyone to hear. Then we provide breakout sessions for volunteers in specific ministry areas from birth through high school. Here, they're able to receive specific training for their areas, cover the calendar, pray for their kids, and build community with their teams.

No matter what size church you come from, this kind of training is something that you could do in your context. And what's so brilliant about gathering all the volunteers together once a year is that it helps them see they're all on the same team—whether they work with babies or high school students.

Creating a single training manual for all volunteers from birth through high school is another great way to ensure that all volunteers hear the same things and understand the same terms and language. If many volunteers in your church move up through the different age levels with the kids they lead, it's helpful to have the same practices and expectations across the board. It takes a little collaboration and makes for a larger manual but ensures clarity for all ages. There's no way I could cover every conceivable topic in a training manual, although my friends will tell you I'd like to try. However, a combination of ideas and practices from different age levels will ensure that we're able to cover the essential bases for the children's and youth ministries while maintaining common language, terms, and best practices throughout.

Keep it simple. Now that we synchronized our team, our calendars, and our training, it's essential that you and I can quickly communicate the essential strategy to parents, volunteers, and other key leaders in our churches. Everyone is busy and we are all barraged with a constant flow of information as we've already discussed. Therefore, in my experience, it's so important we can give a one minute or less overview of what we do. Here's an example of what it can look like:

- **Team of support.** We build a team of support around your child/student by equipping volunteers.
- **Dynamic growth environments.** We create dynamic growth environments (programs) to become the catalyst for next steps at home.
- **Parent equipping.** We equip and empower parents to take next steps at home with their kids.

Now to be clear, this is not *the* strategy, it's simply *a* strategy that I've seen to be effective. For the purpose of this chapter, we will spend some time on unpacking the first two strategies since equipping and empowering has already been covered in prior chapters.

BUILD A TEAM OF SUPPORT AROUND KIDS AND STUDENTS

A number of years ago, I sat down in a Starbucks with youth ministry veteran Mark DeVries after hearing him speak at a local university. (I was following the example of my youth ministry mentor Byron Porisch by networking with and learning from some of the leaders in the field of ministry.) Mark is a fascinating leader with innovative ideas. While in the trenches of ministry, he'd written a number of books. He'd also written a number of articles I'd read about family ministry and how to involve the whole church in investing in the life of a child. As we sat in that coffee house, Mark drew on a napkin a plan for creating a team of support for every child and student in a given church. The premise of the diagram was for children's and youth ministry workers to see themselves as networkers within their local churches, connecting children and students to a wide variety of people who could pour into their lives.

As children's and youth workers, there's a tendency for us to see our roles purely as creators of great environments for kids. Or worse, being the hero to every kid. However, one of the things that's missing when we do that is the opportunity for kids and students to feel a sense of belonging and connection with the church as a whole. As a leader, I've come to realize that I can't be there for every person at every moment. But, just as a sports team works to develop a "deep bench" with as many high-level players as possible at every position, connecting kids with a wide range of adults provides them with a deep bench of people who can offer them support in the moments when they need it most. As Mark DeVries told me, "There are no more Lone Rangers." And he encouraged me to create a culture in my church where kids would have multiple people surrounding them, forming a team of support they could go to whenever they need it. This is one of the first and most crucial steps in creating a healthy family ministry that envisions the whole church—not just those serving in the children's or youth ministries—supporting and equipping the next generation.

Once we've listened to parents and understood their needs, and we have captured their hearts with a vision to partner with them, the next step should be to unpack who they are partnering with specifically. It's not just you and me. It's a team of volunteers and other key influencers to show up in the lives of kids, as well as partner with parents. If those volunteers just show up to run a great program on the weekend or midweek environments, we have missed in a gigantic way. Essentially, their role is to invest in kids and students consistently, get to know the parents (this will take time), and point parents to the next step at home (with the resources you and I provide). And, we know we've accomplished this strategy when volunteers start showing up to soccer games, school plays, and start sending notes in the mail even when they are not asked. (Who sends mail in our world today? Caring adults who want to go the extra mile to show care and intention.)

Greater focus on the team! Here's some great news: I've seen how effective this strategy can be in the lives of kids, students, volunteers, and parents. It's been a long time since I sat down with Mark, and I wish I could say I implemented his strategy with great success since then, but I haven't. Sometimes trial and error are needed to figure out *how* to implement effectively. The great news is in recent years, I've seen parents and volunteers capture the vision, and I've seen kids and students directly impacted by a team of support. Do you want to know what makes it work? It's primarily in the order and the emphasis you give this strategy. Did you notice how building a team of support was first on the list of strategies and the dynamic growth environments (or programs) are mentioned second in order? It's no mistake. Most parents and volunteers will naturally give their attention (if not all of their attention) to the programs we offer. Therefore, we need to elevate the team of support around each child and student. Beginning with a team of support around each child and student points parents (and volunteers) to a much larger biblical strategy. It paints a clear picture we see in Deuteronomy 6:4 when Moses calls the *whole* faith community into reaching the next generation. But, practically speaking, how can this take shape?

One of Five? "What could it look like if every child and student had five key influencers invested in their lives? Five is not a magic number, but can you imagine?" This is the kind of question my friend Heather Sullivan has kept asking for a number of years. It has been questions like this that has led her to develop a strategy to help parents and kids to "find their five" as they consider the key influencers in their faith journey. Simultaneously, volunteers are being trained and equipped to see themselves as one of five in the lives of kids and students. It's also a key part of their training and onboarding as a new volunteer. They don't just show up to run slick ministry programs, they see themselves in partnership with the parents as key influencers on the faith journey of each child and student. Being one of five means showing up consistently in the lives of kids through ministry environments and key milestone moments that we orchestrate in our churches. But it doesn't stop there. We can also encourage parents to identify other key influencers outside of the church who are naturally invested in their kids. These can be other family members, teachers, and coaches who parents consider to be key influencers who can be called into intentional milestones and moments of their child's faith journey. In my experience, sharing the strategy is often all it takes. Parents can quickly identify their team of support and find ways to include them in their child's faith journey with greater intentionality. For Heather, it's a simple strategy calling parents and kids to "find your five," and for volunteers to be trained and empowered to see themselves as "one of five."

CREATE DYNAMIC GROWTH ENVIRONMENTS

Whether you are new to ministry or a veteran, you probably have a good handle on how you run your ministry programs. But, is it possible you could be missing a few essential tweaks that will maximize your impact in partnering with parents and keeping them engaged? What follows are some effective strategies to give you greater impact in your ministry environments while providing parents a clear understanding of how your ministry continues to partner with them.

ENSURE CONSISTENCY BETWEEN AGE LEVELS

If the basic structure and format of your ministries are very different from one age group to another, it can become a stumbling block to helping kids stick around once they move up. Not only is it important for kids to experience things that are familiar from one age level to the next, it's essential to ensure that parents know how things work as well. In the ministries I have led, I've tried to keep as many ministry components between age groups similar as possible so it's not a completely different experience for children and students every time they move up. There's nothing like a sharp ministry left turn to lose kids and families when they move up between programs.

If you are a part of team who provides ministry for birth through high school, it is essential that you are all on the same page as you create the best solutions for families. Sadly, I have heard of good churches with good people who have expended too much sideways energy competing with each other or complaining about the other. Our families are depending on us to collaborate, to communicate, and to lead with humility. If we are not prepared to work as a team to create a unified strategy between ages, then we should probably get a job in the vitamin supplement industry. (I heard they need a little help getting their message out.) Here are a few ideas for ways you can do that in your ministry.

Encourage volunteers to move up. Haley has had Joanna*[3] as her small group leader since she was in third grade. Haley is now entering high school. With all the changes going on in high school it's important that she's able to turn to a small-group leader who knows her and understands how to motivate her when challenges occur. Having Joanna as her small-group leader has often been the difference-maker for Haley, especially during some hard times in middle school.

While not every volunteer can move up with a group of children or students, it's certainly something we encourage whenever possible. Not only is there a great deal of trust built between a caring volunteer like Joanna and Haley, but there's a natural relationship that begins to develop throughout the years between a parent and volunteer. That's a huge win when we can accomplish it. Even a volunteer following kids through a few years will make an incredible difference and be a confidence booster for parents.

Include similar programmatic elements at each age level. In the contexts I have led, I have worked with all ages up through high school. We have a similar structure to our environments at all age levels. It's not that we're trying to take a cookie-cutter approach or be controlling. We just know that kids and parents need some familiarity as their kids move up. Communicating this strategy to parents will help them see you are with them for the long haul and you are considering transition points. For example, the way kids and student's check-in are almost identical. At the beginning of every experience there's a relational connecting time followed by a large-group message and then a small-group experience. Apart from the very smallest ones, every child in our ministry will always experience those three elements every time they gather. There are times in the year that we mix things up and create some alternative elements. But, we know from experience that having similar elements and structures helps our kids stick around and feel comfortable.

Use common language and terms. As simple as it seems, there's great power in establishing a common language. Over time, using common terminology not only helps the team understand where the boat is heading, it also serves to build bridges between age-related environments as parents and kids transition from year to year. For example, if the preschool area is using different terminology than the elementary area, or if the middle school area is using different terminology than the high school area, it can muddy the vision and water down the strategy.

KNOW WHAT KIDS (AND THEIR PARENTS) WANT

Parents are influenced greatly by the opinions of their kids. Every year marketers spend massive amounts of money to capture the attention and commitment of kids, knowing it'll lead to gaining a greater share of the market for their products. I'm not talking about them trying to get kids to buy the latest gadget, figure, or licensed product from the most recent Disney movie. I'm talking about stuff parents buy for themselves. Marketers use kids to influence their parents' purchasing decisions for everything from groceries[4] to cars to apparel.[5] The fact is, marketers know that kids have a great effect on their parents purchasing decisions big and small. And this kind of influence isn't just seen in the world of marketers. If you look closely enough, you'll see how kids are influencing whether or not their parents will buy into your church.

I don't like using the term "buy into" when referring to the local church. For many years, I've struggled with the way some churches have become commercialized, focusing more on numbers than on spiritual health and adopting more of a business mentality than a kingdom mentality. The church isn't supposed to be a business or a marketing machine. But it's essential that we recognize we are in competition for the attention and commitment of kids and parents. Our willingness to engage in that competition can influence a family's decision to attend our church and affect our ability to reach kids with the gospel. When we create ministries that kids love to attend and a strategy that parents can easily commit to, we'll be better able to partner with parents in passing on the faith to the next generation.

What parents want for their kids. "Tell me, what brought you here?" That was the question I asked a single mom a number of years ago as she stood in the lobby of the church with three kids hanging on her legs. Her answer confirmed what I'd observed for some time: it was all about her kids. "I was talking with my friend who started coming here a few months ago. Her kids love coming, and they always have an incredible experience. Your church isn't the kind of church I would normally attend, but I need to be somewhere my kids want to keep coming back to."

After speaking to this mom a little more, I discovered that her church background was quite different from what she had been experiencing at the church her kids loved to keep coming back to. She'd grown up with a traditional background and was more familiar with a liturgical worship service. She had found herself in a church described in the community as "the church with loud music and lights." For someone coming from a background such as this mom had, I can only imagine that it was a bit of shock to the system. But she was allowing herself to get an earache at a new church simply because she thought it was what was best for her kids.

The fact is, parents today are determining where they live and what they do based on what's best for their kids and to give their kids positive feelings and experiences. It's not that parents didn't care before, but we've seen more parents going to greater lengths to ensure their kids are given the finest opportunities in every area of their lives. This isn't always a positive thing, as it can be taken to an extreme. But still, we have to understand that parents are looking to their kids for cues when it comes to where they'll commit. The stereotypical Boomer parents were ultra-focused on their own accomplishments (often to the detriment of their kids). Today, we're seeing the pendulum swing the other way as a greater number of younger parents are investing greater time and resources into their kids' lives. That's true when it comes to faith as well. Even though we meet many parents who don't necessarily know what to say or do in raising their kids with a solid faith, one thing is common: when it comes to the faith of their kids, they're looking for a church their kids love to attend.

Depending on the demographic of the families you work with, many of the parents we work with are also stretched by increasing work pressures and are unable to invest in their kids as much as they'd like. Just recently, I spoke to a single mom who shared that her only hour of solace during the week is at church. While she'd like to provide much more for her kids, she's barely treading water as it is, and she's desperate for support.

Parents like this mom find it hard to see the big picture of investing in their kid's faith since they're living in survival mode most of the time. So often a perceived lack of drive on the part of parents regarding spiritual matters can easily be interpreted as not caring about their child's spiritual journey. But, for many parents, just trying to find a safe place to drop their kids off to learn about God is about as far as they can see. Their efforts to get their kids to church at all can be a great starting point when it comes to partnering with them. As we'll discuss in a later chapter, there will eventually come an opportunity with parents who are constantly living in survival mode for you and I to come alongside them and assist them.

What parents and kids want in your ministry. The way kids and their parents perceive our ministries will determine our ability to effectively partner with parents. But, what does that mean practically speaking? We need to understand what kids (and parents) are looking for and what we need to provide in order to capture their attention as we work to reach and equip them for an exciting faith journey. I'm sure there are plenty of books and blogs out there that'll provide you with some insights on how to create an irresistible ministry. But for our purposes, here's a quick bullet list to help you evaluate your ministry environments in terms of what kids and parents are looking for.

- **Safety.** It doesn't matter if it's a parent of a toddler or a teenager, safety is possibly the most important factor from a parent's perception. A solid check-in and check-out process communicates care and professionalism to parents as they drop their kids off. While it can be frustrating for a parent to fill out registration forms with medical questions or allergy information, it also provides confidence to parents to know that their child's best interests are being looked after. Performing background checks on your volunteers and staff is also critical. Not only does it provide legal protection for your church, but knowing this has been done also gives parents another layer of security and the assurance that they're leaving their kids in good hands.

- **Relationships.** Perhaps the greatest reason children and students return week after week is because a leader has shown care and concern for them and has invested in them. Relationships eventually become the doorway to learning about God. In his book *Purpose-Driven Youth* Ministry, veteran youth worker Doug Fields reports having once heard that "until students are environmentally comfortable, they won't be theologically aware."[6] That's so true. And, establishing positive relationships with kids is a big part of making them feel comfortable.

- **Fun.** From the colors and photos on the walls, to the activities, to the smiles on the faces of volunteers, your environment needs to communicate fun in every way. Having been in a set up and tear down church planting environment, I know how daunting it can be to create engaging environments with few resources. But when leaders and volunteers choose to have more fun than the kids and are the first ones to let their hair down, it's amazing how much it enables the kids to relax and engage as well. With a team of excited volunteers, some fun games, and good lighting, children and students will see your environment as a fun place to learn about God.

- **Experiences.** A change that's occurred in Christian education is the movement away from solely lecture-based learning. Who wants to come and just be talked to? If you consider the most widely used social media and technology[7] they consume, there is a huge element of them being the creators of their digital lives, where they create their brand, producing endless videos, and even their own digital worlds. They want to create and experience life and faith. That's what they do. Speaking to kids and students is not bad, but it will lack fruit in the absence of experiences. Creating some extra time to allow kids to experience a lesson through active learning will help them learn more effectively.

- **Application.** If it doesn't apply to everyday life, it's not likely to keep kids engaged. While some theological concepts can be a little harder to grapple with, it's imperative that you find ways to help kids apply what they're learning. When it's relevant, kids will remember it and put it into practice.

- **Personal Touches.** "If they don't miss me, they must not care." That's what kids and their parents think when no one follows up. Many families have entire seasons away from church. It's essential that someone takes time to follow up with those families and let them know they're missed. Simple things like sending a birthday card or a note of encouragement can make the difference in kids feeling loved and their parents feeling confident in your ministry.

Involve Parents

A common theme I hope you see running through this book is the importance of involving parents in all you do. Not only do parents help you get more accomplished, but they'll also become your biggest advocates and, ultimately, a doorway to partnering with other parents. When parents get involved, they'll treat your ministry as if it's theirs. As a result, they'll catch the biblical vision and, in turn, become the greatest promoters, equippers, and supporters you have of reaching the next generation for Christ.

In my first church ministry, I recruited Ted and his wife to help with snacks and food for the middle school ministry. Ted didn't see himself as a youth leader, but since his boys were involved, this was a good way for him to support them and their youth group. He and his wife faithfully served food and built some great relationships with the students and other youth leaders.

Two years later, we were looking to launch small groups for the first time, and it was proving hard to find good small-group leaders who loved the students and had a desire to shepherd them. With only a week to go, we had one group of seventh-grade boys who did not yet have a small-group leader. So given my limited options, we decided to ask the boys if they had any ideas. (Like I said, our options were limited.) To my amazement, one of the boys instantly mentioned Ted and wanted to know if we could ask him to be their leader. Given my previous conversations with Ted, I was sure he would instantly shoot down the idea if I asked him. But what if one of the boys asked? Genius!

Within a few days, Ted spoke to me and explained that one of the boys had asked him to be their small-group leader. "What did you say, Ted?" I asked. His reply was great. "Well, I couldn't say 'no' to a seventh grader. So I agreed."

I wish I could tell you that Ted is still a small-group leader in the youth ministry today. But, I can't. What I can tell you is that Ted moved from being a parent of a teen, to someone who helped with the food, to a small-group leader and fully invested parent in the ministry for a number of years. Not only did Ted invest in those boys, but he raised the confidence of other parents and became one of our biggest advocates for the youth ministry and its vision.

- **Guidelines for involving parents.** Here are a few practical ideas for getting and keeping parents involved in your ministry.
- **Give them a short job description.** Having a job description for parents lets them know you consider their role important enough to have planned and prepared for it. It will also help them to keep on track and tell when they're successfully accomplishing what you've asked them to do.
- **Share your vision and strategy with them.** When parents get involved, they become part of your team. Sharing vision and strategy helps them to know what the team is trying to accomplish and

how you're trying to accomplish it. Also, once parents get involved in your ministry, they'll often be the first ones to talk to others about its vision and strategy. It's up to you to help them know what to talk about.

- **Create entry steps for them.** Just like Ted, not all parents see themselves as leaders, but they want to help in some way. In my context, some of the easiest ways for parents to get plugged in are by taking on roles such as greeters, snack providers, or setup and tear-down crew members. From there, it's eventually possible for them to step into other leadership responsibilities such as planning events, leading small groups, or even teaching in the large-group gatherings.
- **Ensure their children are comfortable with the arrangement.** For different reasons, not every child wants his or her parents to be closely involved with the group he or she is a part of. In particular, as kids become more self-aware at the preteen age and up, there's often a desire on the part of the kids to have some distance from their parents. It's essential that parents' involvement is a win for both the parents and the kids. If there's a way to involve a parent somewhere behind the scenes, that's often a good way to dispel the embarrassment factor that many kids feel when mom or dad is around.
- **Don't let them parent and serve at the same time.** One of the guidelines I've established for parents who lead in my ministry is that they're not allowed to discipline their own children while ministry activities are going on. If their child needs some redirection or is misbehaving, I ask the parents to get another leader to handle the situation. I set this precedent in order to avoid embarrassment for the kids. Embarrassment and shame can be a big contributor to a child not wanting to come back.

CREATE FAMILY EVENTS

As I mentioned early on in the book, there's a tendency for us, as children's and student workers, to stay focused on kids and not consider partnering with parents. In a similar way, I think we can tend to focus on kids and parents separately and not think about how we can minister to families as a whole. When that happens, we miss opportunities to bring families together in ways that enable parents and kids to continue conversations about faith at home. We also miss opportunities to help parents meet and connect with the parents of other kids in our ministries. There are times when family members need to worship and learn in age-specific ways, but there's also a balance to be found in bringing parents and their children together, too.

Here are some examples of events you could consider for your context:

- **Family movie night.** Elementary-age kids and their parents come in pj's for pizza and a fun kids' movie.
- **Parent/student rake and run.** Students and parents go out into the community to rake leaves and do basic yard work for single moms and widows, working quickly at each location and then moving on to the next.
- **Family crafts and carols.** Kids from birth through elementary age make crafts and sing Christmas carols for the sweet folks at a local nursing home.
- **Operation Christmas Child event.** Parents and kids work together to buy toys, toiletries, and school supplies and pack them in shoeboxes to be sent to kids overseas through the ministry of Samaritan's Purse.
- **Family game show night.** Middle school and high school students invite their parents to a game show night where parents got to be the heroes (or goofs) on stage with students. Lots of laughter and fun!
- **Parent/student transition events.** Kids move from elementary school to middle school, and then middle school to high school. Creating an event for students to experience their new environment and inviting their parents to join for all or part of it can be a game changer. It's another opportunity to share vision and strategy with parents too. In my experience, as long as you manage carefully just how much parents and kids are together (it's less as they get older if you haven't figured out) it can be a huge win for students, parents, and the volunteers who are moving up with them. It's also good to

have a focused time to equip parents in a new phase of parenting, as well as share the vision and strategy with them.

There are many other great ways to hold family events that create memories and enable families to continue their conversations at home.

What works for you? These examples are just some of the things that have worked for me. Quite honestly as you can see, there is no rocket science behind them, just a goal to help families to celebrate together, learn together, and serve together. Keep in mind that these events were done over a number of years. And less is always more as they say. If you were to create just one family event this year, that's a great start. I would strongly suggest a yearly transition event. Remember to involve parents in the creation of events like these. Consider their ideas as a starting place for what will truly work. An idea that seems only average can have an incredible outcome when parents are behind it. At the same time, an incredible idea might only see an average outcome if you're trying to do it all on your own.

Schedule What Works for Parents, Not Just for You

One of the areas you and I need to be more and more strategic with is how we schedule activities and events. The prioritization of church activities isn't like it used to be back in the old days, when the average church family would come to Sunday morning service, Sunday evening service, and a midweek activity. (I never did that myself, but I'm told it's the way it used to be.)

The average family today has a plethora of options on any given week. Given the reality of packed schedules and extra-curricular activities, it's essential to have a schedule for your ministry that's easy for parents to work into and stick with. For most children's ministries, it's easy to predict that Sunday morning services will work for parents. But what about events, parent workshops, or volunteer training times? We need to find a way to schedule those things so we're not conflicting with parents' schedules any more than we have to. Here are some quick tips for what's helped us do that in our context:

- Survey parents to get a gauge for what days and times work best for them and schedule events accordingly.
- Schedule well in advance and communicate dates for special events 8-10 weeks out.
- Don't schedule events during typically busy seasons for parents, such as the first four weeks of school, the end of school, or the beginning of summer. These are times parents will thank you for a lighter schedule.
- Try to use your facility in a way that allows you to have multiple groups meeting on campus on the same night. For example, our middle school and high school ministries meet on Wednesdays during the same time slot but in different places in the building.
- Avoid days and times that are considered to be "family times." We moved our high school ministry away from Sunday evenings because many of our parents told us it was their only evening of the week for family time.
- For parent training events, try to have them at times parents are already on-site. Either get permission to meet with parents during services for one-off training events, or at the least disruptive time. Don't make parents come out another night of the week when weeknights are already at a premium and parents might have to line up additional childcare.

The strategies you use in your ministry serve as important steps toward seeing your vision of partnering with parents become a reality. Among other things, they build confidence and trust as parents see progress made toward the goal of reaching and equipping their kids for Christ. The strategies outlined in this chapter are only a few of the ones you'll want to include. There are likely others you can add that'll be specific to your context. Take some time to consider what strategies are most essential for you. Write them down, keep them simple, repeatable, and recruit parents and volunteers to help you share the strategy.

GAME SUMMARY

To effectively partner with parents, we must have a clear strategy for reaching and equipping kids that's easy for parents to see in action.

PRACTICE DRILLS

1. On a scale of 1 to 5—with 1 being "no one even has their oars in" and 5 being "all oars are in and rowing in the same direction"—rate your church or ministry on whether it has a synchronized team approach. Without apportioning blame to any one person or area, list some of the barriers that keep your ministry from functioning as a synchronized team. Then identify some ways you can work toward becoming a synchronized team.

2. Divide a page into two columns. On one side, list the elements that are consistent for the children and students in your ministry as they move through the age groups. On the other side, list the elements that are different from one age level to the next. Get together with a few of the key players in your children's and youth ministries and brainstorm ways you could make the elements that are different more consistent throughout all the age groups.

3. Review the list of things kids and parents are looking for in children's and youth ministry environments on page XX. Create a quick survey to find out how parents would rate your church or ministry in each of those areas. Assemble a group of parents and ministry leaders or volunteers to help you interpret the results of the survey. Include parents new to your ministry in this group to ensure a fresh perspective is represented.

4. Create a list of roles for parents who want to get involved in your ministry (including roles that might already be filled by parents or other volunteers). Write a basic job description for each role. Discuss the appropriate job description with those who are already serving in your ministry, affirming their value to you and the ministry and thanking them for their service. Identify parents who could fill roles that aren't currently filled, discuss with them the job description for

that role, and invite them to get involved (this could include asking parents who are already serving to move into a position of greater responsibility, if you think they're ready).

5. Sit down with two or three parents and brainstorm some family events that you can do in the coming year. Choose one event to begin planning, get it on your calendar, and ask your parent brainstorming team to help you make it happen.

6. Evaluate your ministry calendar in terms of how you think it adds to or alleviates stress in parents' schedules. Look at the list of scheduling tips on page XX. Choose one you think is especially helpful, and apply it to your calendar.

Endnotes

[1] Julie Straw, Mark Scullard, Susie Kukkonen, and Barry Davis, *The Work of Leaders: How Vision, Alignment, and Execution Will Change the Way You Lead*, (San Francisco: Wiley Publishers, 2013), p. 5.

[2] Coxwain (Rowing). http://www.usrowing.org/Libraries/Coaching/Common_Rowing_Vocabulary.sflb.ashx. Accessed April 17, 2015.

[3] *Names have been changed.

[4] Jennifer L. Harris Ph.D, *Kids Under the Influence: The psychology of marketing to young consumers.* http://www.psychologytoday.com/blog/kids-under-the-influence/201402/what-s-parent-do. Accessed December 5, 2014.

[5] Natalie Nahai, *5 Things You Need To Know About Marketing to Generation Y*, http://www.psychologytoday.com/blog/webs-influence/201305/5-things-you-need-know-about-marketing-gen-y. Accessed December 5, 2014.

[6] Doug Fields, *Purpose-Driven Youth Ministry: 9 Essential Foundations for Healthy Growth* (Grand Rapids: Zondervan Publishing House, 1998), 118.

[7] https://www.pewresearch.org/internet/2018/05/31/teens-social-media-technology-2018/. Accessed August 14, 2020.

Chapter 9

POINT TO IMPORTANT MILESTONES

HOW TO HELP PARENTS AND KIDS KNOW THEY'RE HEADING DOWN THE RIGHT ROAD.

Shortly after I graduated from high school, I took a road trip with my good friend Martin. We had much in common, such as our love of soccer and music, but we also shared a similar faith journey. Both of us grew up outside the church and were invited by friends to the same local youth group. Martin and I came to Christ at the same time and were baptized on the same day. But, when we graduated from high school, he went off to university while I stayed home and worked. It was a tough time for me personally, since I felt like most of my good friends—like Martin—had left for an exciting life at university while I worked in a boring accounts department.

I'm an extravert. And accounting is an extravert's nightmare. I hate numbers and love people. Anytime I could get away to catch up with my friends, I'd jump in my rusty Ford Fiesta for a road trip. (I love taking road trips, too!) Once, while Martin was back on winter break, he asked if I could drive him back to his university to pick up some important books he needed over the break. It was a great opportunity to hang out with Martin and get to see his new life at university. So we set off on a cold, January morning with our destination in sight...or so I thought.

It took us about two hours to navigate around the M25, which is a circular freeway that circumvents the whole city of London. (At rush hour, I like to call it the largest circular parking lot in the world.) We were excited when we saw signs for the exit leading us to Reading University, where Martin went to school. I'd never been to the city of Reading before, but of course Martin had been there many times by now. I had no reason to doubt his navigation, and I was sure that the next part of our journey would be a whole lot easier than the crawl of the M25.

Before long we were heading up the M40 motorway, enjoying each other's company and the rolling hills of the English countryside. About an hour later, I began to see snow on top of the hills and more and more sheep around us. While I loved looking at the rolling hills of England, I didn't like what the snow and sheep indicated about the direction we were heading. It was the road sign telling us that Birmingham was only eighty miles away that made us realize we were, indeed, heading in the wrong direction. Reading is due west of London. Seeing signs for Birmingham told us we were clearly heading northwest. It wasn't long before we came to discover what the problem was: Reading is just off the M4 motorway, not the M40. (If only we would've had a GPS back then.)

While Martin and I had a destination in mind, we didn't have a map to help us evaluate our progress on the journey. I knew that Birmingham wasn't near Reading, but we still travelled a long way up the freeway admiring the snow covered hills and sheep, when we could have already been at our destination. In a similar way, parents often know where their kids need to get to in their faith journeys and have every intention of helping them get there, but they don't always know what to look for to help their kids confirm they're on the right path.

WHY MILESTONES ARE IMPORTANT

In Chapter 4, we talked about the importance of casting for parents the biblical vision for raising their children with a strong faith foundation. Casting such a vision helps parents see the big picture of the faith journey their children are on, like showing them the destination on a road map. However, it's also important that we help parents identify the particular routes their children need to take to get to that destination, marking out where and what direction their kids need to turn to be successful on their journeys. We do that, in part, by helping them to see the crucial milestones to watch for. If a clear biblical vision is a destination for parents to head toward, milestones serve as strategic markers along the way.

In his book *Shift—What it Takes to Finally Reach Families Today*, Brian Haynes talks about the milestones his church focuses on, saying,

> These milestones serve as markers of progression on the spiritual formation journey. When a person reaches a milestone, that growth is celebrated as a praise for how God is working in the person and as a motivation to continue walking the path.[1]

That's a great description of what milestones are and how to best interact with them.

Without milestones, many parents end up sending their kids on a journey in the wrong direction without realizing it. Their kids experience a lot of good things along the way, but they're also ill-equipped for the long haul ahead. The parents you and I will meet will often have the right intentions for their children but will also be taking them in the wrong direction, missing crucial milestones along the way. I can't tell you how many parents I meet who look back and see many missed opportunities to intentionally invest in their child's faith journey. Most of them sincerely care about their kids and wanted to help them become successful in life and faith. However, in their attempt to raise well-rounded, successful kids, they got swept along in a tide of extra-curricular activities and missed opportunities to bring faith into focus and incorporate faith into everyday life.

Parents may be in the driver's seat, but we can't assume they always know where they're heading or how to get there. As quickly as they hear and agree with the vision to raise their kids with a solid faith foundation, they're back to their day-to-day journeys of parenting in survival mode. Instead of becoming annoying "back seat drivers," we need to come alongside parents as helpful navigators. We need to point them to crucial milestones that'll help them keep their kids on track to developing a solid faith foundation.

> Instead of becoming annoying "back seat drivers," we need to come alongside them as helpful navigators.

FOCUS ON WHAT MATTERS MOST

Not all milestones look the same. The milestones you point parents toward will depend, in part, on the denominational background you're a part of. My journey of faith and ministry has taken me on a varied denominational path that's enabled me to understand and appreciate the unique qualities of a number of denominations. I've had the privilege of attending or ministering in Anglican, Baptist, Lutheran, Evangelical Covenant, Wesleyan, and non-denominational churches. (If I missed your denomination, don't worry, it seems as though I'm working my way toward it at some point.) My wife's family is Roman Catholic, and I'm well-connected with friends who are in ministry roles in all kinds of denominational backgrounds. As you'd expect, I do have my doctrinal convictions. But I also love the theological diversity that can be found in the church today.

That being said, you might not agree with all the milestones I'm suggesting. But it's essential that you apply the principle of helping parents identify important milestones in your context. Don't get hung up on whether you agree with the particular milestones themselves. Rather, consider your unique denominational identity, and look for milestones that parents in your ministry can easily follow and apply in their family situations.

HOW TO INCORPORATE MILESTONES IN YOUR MINISTRY

Earlier, I mentioned Brian Haynes' book *Shift—What it Takes to Finally Reach Families Today*. In it, he outlines a number of steps that his church takes with parents in their milestones strategy.[2] The items in the list below are adapted from the steps Haynes has identified and offer three basic ideas for incorporating an emphasis on milestones in your ministry.

- **Core teaching.** For every milestone, provide parents (and their children) with a practical and biblical teaching that focuses on: (1) the significance of the milestone, (2) how God has been faithful and present up until now, (3) preparation for the next part of the child's journey. This can be offered in a formal class, a booklet, or as a handout.
- **Cues for parents.** To reinforce the teaching, give parents a number of ways to continue the conversation at home with their kids. These can include conversation starters and activities that focus again on the significance of the milestone, God's presence and faithfulness, and preparation for the next steps.
- **Celebration.** Whether it's a church event or something parents create for their child at home, celebrate each milestone when the child reaches it. This could involve anything from a dinner at the child's favorite restaurant to a father/son or mother/daughter getaway. Suggest ideas to parents like writing a letter to their child or giving the child a gift that's symbolic of the particular milestone he or she has reached as a way to emphasize its significance.

There are many more things you and I could do to implement effective milestones, but it's important to take one step at a time. Not only are your parents and kids on a journey of faith that requires them to take one step at a time, but we also must not forget that implementing milestones might require you take one step at a time. When I first started to consider what I could do to point parents to milestones, I wanted to change the world all at once. I wanted to create parent seminars for each milestone, and I had ideas for all kinds of elaborate celebrations for parents and kids. However, I've learned (and am learning) that it's better to implement a few simple ideas, get them established and sustainable, and then move on to something more. So often there's a tendency to want to do it all at once. But, that's not sustainable for us, and it's not likely to be implemented well.

One thing I have found to be helpful is to work with parents to create a "map" of the journey they and their kids are on with the essential milestones marked along the way. It can be a one-page sheet that looks like an actual road map (if you're the creative type) or something as simple as a chart or list of key milestones. Creating a map can be a helpful way for you and them to visualize the journey they're on, especially as they consider the next steps that are coming along. Perhaps the most important part of such a map is including a specific destination for who parents want their children to become. That destination will ultimately dictate the direction they guide their kids and influence their level of determination to watch for the critical milestones.

Other elements to include in a map of milestones are:

- The name of each milestone from pre-birth to adulthood
- A one-sentence description of the milestone's significance
- Space for parents to write a one-sentence, developmental description of the child at each milestone (where the child's development was for milestones that have already passed or where they hope the child's development will be for milestones yet to come)
- Space for parents to describe how God was present and faithful up to that point (for milestones the child has already reached)
- A one-sentence description of what's ahead for the child and how he or she can begin preparing for the next milestone to come.

CRITICAL MILESTONES

Moses' words in Deuteronomy 6:4-9 provided the people of Israel a roadmap for incorporating faith into everyday living. He encouraged parents to communicate faith to their children in the teachable moments of everyday living and also by creating intentional faith traditions that would help their children remember the commandments God had given. Those are the same things we want to encourage parents to do when we point them to important milestones. With that in mind, let's look at two specific types of milestones that are significant in the lives of parents and their children: faith milestones and life milestones.

Faith milestones are rooted in biblical tradition and focus. They point to commitment and deepening faith steps that children or their parents will take on their faith journeys. They also celebrate and point to all that God is doing and has done in the life of a child and his or her family. Depending on your denominational background, faith milestones could include (but are not limited to) things such as dedication, salvation, communion, baptism, or confirmation. While these milestones aren't directly connected to the different life milestones we'll look at later, faith in general—to which these milestones point—has a significant overlap with and influence on those other milestones. That's why I've mentioned them first. As most denominations provide their own teaching on these kinds of milestones, along with a format for celebrating those that they practice, much of what you need to incorporate faith milestones into your ministry may already be in place.

Life milestones are turning points that occur naturally and normally in the daily, weekly, monthly, and yearly activities of parents and their kids. As they encounter these moments, it's essential to create milestones that celebrate what God has done and invite him into the next phase of the journey. Usually these are times that every child or adult will look back on as defining moments in their lives. In their book *The Power of Moments*, Chip and Dan Heath refer to these moments as "transition moments."[3] From starting school to entering adulthood, there are certain turning points in life where we all need to put a stake in the ground, acknowledging God's work thus far and looking forward to the journey ahead with him. For many parents and children, these natural and normal turning points often offer little or no acknowledgement of what God has done or is doing. It's our job to help parents take specific and strategic steps to create milestones that point them and their children to what God has done and is doing. The following is a list of six life milestones I would suggest. You're welcome to add more to this list. The key is finding significant turning points in the life of a child or parent, and then including faith into these times.

Birth. It's definitely a milestone when a child is conceived and parents start looking forward to the child's birth. Consider the amount of time and resources first-time parents pour into preparing for the arrival of their child. At this stage, they're typically very focused and determined to do whatever it takes to set up their child for success. It's not that parents don't care when second and third children come along. The first child just provides a greater degree of first-time learning and experience. Just consider the amount of time, energy, and money that goes into decorating the baby's room and buying the cutest clothes for a first child. Consider the amount of reading and education a first-time parent is willing to invest in. The fact is, a first-time parent is more receptive to learn than at any other time. I still remember reluctantly attending a birth class with Lisa for a couple of weeks and reading a book "for guys" about being a new father. (I remember that it had just enough macho stories to keep me interested.) The reality for us in ministry is that the church has more opportunity to speak into the lives of expecting parents than at any other time of the parenting journey. So often we begin conversations about faith formation after the baby is born, when the parents are exhausted and already on the path to survival mode. Meeting with and investing in parents who are expecting their first child is perhaps the best opportunity to help them create a faith map with strategic milestones. In some respects, it's like mapping out a journey prior to getting in the car and heading off down the road. It's so much better to figure out the routes and milestones before the journey starts than to get lost in the winding roads and fog of parenting not knowing how to get back on track.

The start of school. The first day of school is always a big deal. It can be scary and exciting all at the same time. There's a flurry of activity around shopping for new clothes and school supplies and getting kids a new haircut so they look good for their first big day. There are also the anxieties kids and parents can experience: for kids, the uncertainty that comes with new teachers, new classrooms, or even new classmates; for parents, the fretfulness of wanting their kids to succeed but knowing they're losing a measure of control. At this significant turning point in the life of a child (and his or her parents), creating a milestone is a powerful way to remind them both of how God has been with them and helped them in the past, and that He will continue to be with them in the years ahead.

Puberty. I used to sit on a reproductive health committee for my local school system. It was comprised of parents, teachers, community leaders, and a solitary pastor (that was me). Part of our role was to oversee what curriculum makes it into the classroom and at what ages kids are deemed ready to receive certain aspects of sex education. What I really appreciated about the committee was its focus on partnering with parents and allowing parents to be the ones who share vital information with their kids. My experience on this committee has made me even more committed to assist and support parents as they reach this milestone, celebrating the changes in their child's life while also giving them a healthy road map for their relationships now and in the future. For most parents, talking about sexuality and relationships can be very awkward and unnerving. However, there's too much at stake for parents not to have these conversations. Given the choice of allowing culture to dictate their child's view on sexuality or having that talk themselves, most parents will choose to get over their apprehensions. In a world that's increasingly over-sexualized, it's essential that we empower and equip parents to help their kids discover God's best for sex and relationships. When we provide parents with resources and helpful teaching on the topic, it has a positive effect on their kids' lives.

Adolescence. Let me just say it: adolescence is messy! As I write this, I have a teenager in my house and a pre-teen following close behind. I can attest to the confusion and struggle that both parents and students go through in this precarious time of life. From my experience working with students, I can also attest to the relief both parties experience when they turn the corner out of adolescence and look back to see how God has helped them navigate the joys and the challenges in this season of life. I compare adolescence to driving down a winding country lane in England on a foggy day. You never know what's coming around the corner, and the direction seems to be ever-changing from one moment to the next. Therefore, given what children and parents are about to enter into as they encounter adolescence, it's essential that we help them develop some realistic expectations and helpful tools for the journey ahead.

Graduation. Growing up in England meant that I never saw a great deal of celebration for this life milestone. While it's changed a little in the UK, most kids don't have a graduation party or receive cards or gifts like they do in the United States. Perhaps it's because we Brits are too focused on the end of the soccer season at that time of year? Regardless of what my fellow Brits do, I know that here in the United States, graduation is a big deal. And given that students and parents place such a big emphasis on congratulating and celebrating, it's important that we help them to bring a spiritual emphasis to the celebration. By doing so, we enable them to give God the glory and to look ahead as they continue their journey with their heavenly father.

Many churches set aside a Sunday to celebrate their high school graduates. In the past few years, I've asked to preach in the main service that day, and I've created a sermon that's relevant to graduates and also applicable to everyone else. It's another way I've used to focus on the significance of this milestone, to emphasize how God has been present and faithful, and to prepare graduating students (and their parents) for the next part of the journey. It's also a great way to encourage church members to support parents and students as they transition into a new season of life.

HELPING GRADUATES CELEBRATE

Here are some additional things your church can do to make a graduation Sunday especially meaningful for students and their parents.

- Give graduating students a gift with a practical and spiritual emphasis, such as a Bible, a devotional book, or spiritually uplifting music.
- Have parents write a letter to their graduating students to affirm their accomplishment and offer to let them read it during the service.
- Let students display a photo collage for church members to look at before and after the service.
- Pair students and their parents with a prayer partner at church—someone who will check-in with and pray for the student and family regularly.
- Have a photographer take photos of students with their parents, small-group leaders, and church staff where applicable, and send the pictures to the family.
- Invite a youth ministry volunteer or a prominent church leader to pray for graduating students during the service.
- Commission students to minister wherever the next season of life is taking them (college, the military, the workforce, etc.)

Adulthood. Some people are now advising that adolescence isn't complete until individuals reach their mid-twenties.[4] Consequently, adulthood can feel like it's a long way off for some students. However, the transition to adulthood doesn't necessarily correspond with graduation from high school. For some, it can come later. For others, it can come sooner. Developmentally, most students will not have fully attained the status of adult. (My wife maintains that I have yet to attain this myself.) But it's essential to provide some strategic steps to help students enter into this next stage of their lives, regardless of their age.

When we lived in Michigan, most years my family headed to West Michigan for our summer vacation. The love the Lake Michigan fresh water and the beaches. They are pristine and clean and the sand even "squeaks" when you walk on it, (yes, you read that correctly—It has something to do with the mineral content in the sand). We also love to see our good friends, Troy and Amy. We usually end up hanging out with them at our favorite beach, having a blast swimming with the kids while I get sunburned on my pasty, English skin. We've spent hours together and I love being with Troy who has a humble wisdom that's been developed from an authentic faith walk.

A number of years ago when we were in West Michigan, both of Troy's teenage boys were getting ready to head out to college, leaving Amy and him to be empty nesters. But before his boys left for college, Troy wanted to create a milestone for them that would be etched in their memories for many years to come. Months prior, he asked his boys to write down the names of Christian men who had influenced their lives, what about each of those men had influenced them, and how they saw Christ in each of those men. Without the boys knowing it, he sent their notes to the men they identified and invited each of them to a dinner where they would pray for the boys, share their collective wisdom, and give them God-honoring advice for the future.

One summer evening, the boys arrived at a beautiful house overlooking Lake Michigan, only having been told to dress up a little and to come hungry. When they arrived, they were blown away to see the men whose names they had written down and talked with Troy about just a few months previously. After dinner, a time of sharing, and a time of prayer, Troy's sons were each presented with a large, wood-framed mirror that was engraved on the outside with some words to remind them in the years to come that they were men of God, called to walk steadfastly in the faith and to reflect Christ to everyone. Troy's sons arrived at that house as boys on a journey. But once they encountered this milestone, they were ready to move into adulthood as young Christian men, commissioned by their father and a group of godly men.

Troy's idea has been emulated many times by his friends. It would be a great way for parents you know to help their kids step into adulthood too. Or perhaps you might even use it yourself.

OTHER MILESTONES

In speaking with other friends of mine who are in ministry, I've come across some other areas that are helpful to have milestones created around. The following ideas don't lend themselves to merging life and faith as easily. But, it's crucial to see these life issues as areas where children and students greatly need the kind of direction that comes from experiencing a milestone event. Anytime a parent can apply faith to these issues is an opportunity to make faith stick in a greater way.

Technology & media milestones. Kids are getting into technology at a younger age and are exposed to more and more in the media all the time. If parents aren't careful to create some kind of media milestone for their kids, it's very possible that at some point they'll all pay the price. An example of creating a milestone around the use of media and technology would be having kids sign a media contract. A media contract defines the terms of appropriate technology usage and enables parents to come alongside their children and talk about wise decisions, guarding their hearts, and moderation. It also enables parents to call their kids to a greater level of responsibility in their lives.

Driving milestones. What kid can't wait to drive? Alright, there might be a few who prefer riding horseback. But most kids can't wait for the day they get their driver's license. It's a bit of a milestone in itself. Parents can add to the significance of the event by coming alongside of their child with something like a parent-teen driving agreement. As with a media contract, a driving agreement gives parents an opportunity to talk with their children about wise decisions and challenges students with an even greater sense of responsibility. Organizations like the Center for Disease Control (cdc.gov) have printable driving agreements parents can use or adapt to include elements of faith.

Money milestones. Once students have the ability to make their own money, it's a great time for parents to create a milestone event that allows them to come alongside their kids and talk about financial responsibility. As students take a step toward adulthood and greater independence, parents can support and equip them with some basic biblical principles for managing money, such as tithing, saving, and spending wisely. One idea for doing this is for parents to let their child earn money by working around the home in some way. The work should be separate from the child's normal chores, and the amount earned should be separate from any regular allowance he or she receives. When the work is done and the child has been paid, the parents and child can set up a time to go out and spend the money under the following guidelines: the child has to give ten percent of what he or she has earned to the church first, save ten percent, and spend at least part of what's left on someone else, such as buying something for a sibling or a friend. Then, the parents could celebrate with their child by taking him or her out for a meal at his or her favorite restaurant (or even for just an ice cream cone, if that's all the parents' finances will allow).

MAKE MILESTONES STAND OUT

Years ago, before we had kids, Lisa and I backpacked around Europe one summer. (Did I tell you that I love to travel?) One of our favorite countries to visit was Ireland. There's just something about the Emerald Isle that's wonderful and relaxing. It was also quite an adventure driving on the country roads. We nearly ran over several sheep and sheep dogs along the way, and I'm surprised we didn't get lost more than we did. You see, in that part of the country, road signs, markers, and milestones aren't really designed to stand out. They just sort of blend in to the surroundings. (When we arrived back in the States, it was like the road signs were shouting at us.) If it weren't for my highly trained and observant navigator—Lisa—we would've been perpetually lost.

Milestones in the faith journey of a child should be a big deal. They should be monuments children and parents create together to celebrate all God has done and to look forward to all He will do. Anytime you and I can help parents provide directions and navigational markers for their child, it'll be a defining moment for both of them.

GAME SUMMARY

By pointing parents to milestones in their kids' lives, we help both of them evaluate where they are now and whether they're on track to get where they want to go.

PRACTICE DRILLS

1. Take some time to journal about the milestones you've experienced in your own life. In what ways were your parents involved in those milestones? What lessons from your experiences with milestones could help you point out milestones parents should be watching for in their kids' lives?

2. Create a list of the milestones your church helps kids and parents celebrate? Include both faith and life milestones. What milestones could you add to this list in the future?

3. Choose one milestone to start pointing parents to right away. Begin developing a core teaching, some parent cues, and a celebration to help parents highlight that milestone in their child's life.

4. Create a "map" of the journey parents and their kids are on, marking significant milestones along the way from birth through adulthood. You might also recruit an artistically-gifted parent to create a pictorial version of your map. Regardless of the form your "map" takes, leave space for parents to add in notes about their child's development at each milestone and ways God has been present and faithful.

Endnotes

[1] Brian Haynes, *Shift—What it Takes to Finally Reach Families Today*, (Loveland: Group Publishing, 2009), 42.

[2] Ibid, 42.

[3] Chip Heath and Dan Heath, *The Power of Moments: Why Certain Experiences Have Extraordinary Impact*, (New York: Simon & Schuster, 2017), 44.

[4] http://www.bbc.com/news/magazine-24173194.

Chapter 10

HELP OUT IN HARD TIMES

HOW HELPING FAMILIES IN DIFFICULTY OPENS THE DOOR FOR PARTNERING WITH PARENTS.

laire's* baby wasn't supposed to make it. About halfway through the pregnancy, she received the devastating news that her baby had an extremely rare chromosomal disorder that would likely result in the baby not making it to full term. There had only been a handful of documented cases of this disorder. And in the unlikely event that the baby did make it full term, only two babies with the disorder had ever survived. It was extremely difficult news to comprehend. And it was painfully hard to explain to her elementary-age daughter, who was elated about becoming a big sister. Claire had been away from church for a while, and Lisa and I didn't know her and her daughter that well. But we felt compelled to come alongside her and see what we could do to help her through this gut-wrenching time.

The weeks passed quickly, and it seemed that the baby was making fairly normal progress. It was also amazing to see how God was giving Claire strength and comfort each day, despite the great uncertainty that lay ahead. It wasn't long before the doctors planned to induce Claire in the hope they could give the baby a greater chance of survival. With all that I knew about the situation, the pessimist in me didn't expect the baby to make it through the birth. I was already thinking about how to best comfort the family. But in that time, I also sensed God redirecting my energy to pray for a miracle and for this little baby to live.

To everyone's amazement and joy, Claire had a beautiful baby girl who at the time was only one of three babies with this condition to survive past birth. When Lisa and I arrived at the hospital to meet this little miracle, it was wonderful to see Claire with a beaming smile, full of God-given confidence. Her little girl will have many special needs in her lifetime. But it was so fulfilling to be a part of their journey and to help Claire and her older daughter find hope and support in our church family.

Just a few weeks after the baby was born, the church had an incredible weeklong camp for elementary-age kids that I thought Claire's older daughter would love. When I didn't see her name on the registration list, I wasn't surprised. I knew Claire was living in survival mode. She was getting meals from the church, and various family and friends were supporting her. All this was entirely new territory for her, and every minute of her day was occupied with doctors' visits, caring for a baby with special needs, and looking after her other daughter. Eventually I was able to make contact. I got her older daughter registered for the camp and invited Claire to come to coffee time every morning for the moms of the campers. I didn't expect her to have time, but I hoped we could get her better connected with some of the great women at our church. To my amazement, she came every day. It was during that time that she had some great conversations, including one with another mom who had a child with special needs.

Claire eventually joined a Bible study for moms of children with special needs where she experienced the love and support of a group of women who understood and cared for her. Until we moved to North Carolina, Lisa and I used to see her every week at church, and she often would stop by our home with her little miracle to hang out with Lisa while her elder daughter had play dates with one of our kids.

LESSONS FROM HELPING HURTING PARENTS

One of the most significant ways you and I can begin to partner with parents is to support them in hard times. There are parents in our ministries who—like Claire—are going through challenging times and feel alone in their predicament. Their circumstances may not be as dramatic as Claire's, but they're difficult nonetheless. When we seize the opportunity to come alongside these parents, it not only meets their need in the moment; it can open the door to supporting and equipping them in other ways in the future.

While every situation is different, let me share some helpful lessons from my experience with helping Claire and other parents like her. As you navigate through these points, be thinking and praying about specific parents in your ministry you could come alongside of in greater ways.

Be attentive. Coming alongside parents when they're facing difficult situations requires us to be alert to what's going on in their lives and to be intentional about offering them support. The challenge for many of us is that we're sometimes too focused on our programs to be aware of the people around us. Consequently, we don't always do very well with offering support either. On the other hand, many parents do a good job of hiding their struggles. They come to church and drop their kids off with what I refer to as "fake church smiles." They offer a cordial "good morning" or "hello," but there can be a lot more going on inside. Not every situation is as complex and unique as Claire's, but you can be sure that every family you come into contact with is navigating its own challenging situations at times. It's essential that you and I are as attentive as possible and recognize those challenging situations as God-given opportunities to come alongside of and partner with parents.

Communicate with your team. It's impossible for one person to see all the needs of the families that come to your church. That's why it's so important to have a system of communication that ensures you and your team (staff and volunteers) can share with each other what you're seeing. There are times I would be completely unaware of a hardship a family is facing unless another staff member was able to clue me in on it.

Create a system for communicating the needs you see in your weekly meetings and share any concerns or prayer requests you have for families facing adversity. Then discuss what would be the appropriate ways for you to assist in those situations.

With all that in mind, it's also imperative that each person on your team understands the expectation of maintaining confidentiality regarding those things that are shared. Don't let the communication of information within your team become a source of gossip or embarrassment to the families you minister to.

Work with others. Just as it's impossible to know all that's occurring in the life of a family, it's also impossible for one person to attend to every need. It's necessary that we all take a team approach and spread out the load of care and support. In the case of Claire, the care ministries director was able to orchestrate meeting her practical needs and our small-groups coordinator focused on getting her connected with the moms' Bible study. I was able to get her connected with other parents by lining up play dates for her oldest daughter in addition to the time they spent with Lisa and our kids. In the course of a year, there were four or more people who played a key role in seeing Claire get connected, find support, and grow deeper in her relationship with God. And, her two kids are benefitting from a mom who feels hopeful about the future and is making faith a huge priority these days.

Connect parents with experts. In the chapter on providing resources to parents, we talked about how crucial it is to develop a list of experts in your church or community that can help parents and their kids. Knowing the names of some good counselors, doctors, or other professionals with expertise on children and the family will be something for which parents facing hard times will be forever thankful.

There are a lot of parents who'll never allow you into their lives while they're living life in the fast lane and their kids are doing reasonably well. However, there will often be opportunities where parents or their kids find themselves lost on the highway of life and in need of help and support. It's in these moments that an attentive and caring person like you or me can come alongside them and make a real difference. Seizing those opportunities will not only help them deal with whatever pain they're experiencing at that time, but could also open doors to continue partnering with them on their journeys down the road.

GAME SUMMARY

Seizing the opportunity to help parents facing hard times can become an entry point to partnering with them in their parenting journeys.

PRACTICE DRILLS

1. List your top barriers to being aware of difficulties in the lives of the families to whom you minister. Brainstorm some ways you can overcome those barriers, and choose one of those ways to put into practice.

2. At your next regular ministry team meeting, ask, "Which families in our congregation are struggling or experiencing some kind of pain?" Then, discuss appropriate ways to offer help or comfort to the families that are mentioned. Assign members of your team to lead the efforts in helping each family mentioned.

3. Write down the primary ways in which you and your team communicate family hardships that arise in your church. Meet with your team and discuss ways you could improve communication to ensure that you're not missing opportunities to assist and support parents in need.

4. Create a list of people in your church who could provide practical, spiritual, and emotional support to parents. Contact those people, and ask their permission to give their names out, as necessary, to parents you think they could be of help to.

5. As a way to familiarize yourself with the family support options available through your church, ask the person who oversees the congregational care of your church (this could be your pastor, a staff member, or a volunteer) to share with you their process for caring for families dealing with difficult circumstances.

Endnote

* Name has been changed.

BUILD A TEAM OF SUPPORT FOR PARENTS

THE IMPORTANCE OF CONNECTING PARENTS WITH OTHERS WHO CAN PARTNER WITH THEM AS WELL.

As we've already discussed, it's essential to build a team of support around kids and students as well as to communicate and train parents and volunteers in this key strategy. When key volunteers invest in kids, while seeing themselves as "in it together" with parents, we then begin to see a picture of Deuteronomy 6:4 come into being as the whole faith community reaches the next generation. But it's possible to miss a key component of building a team of support. What about parents? Do they need a team of support too?

For many years, I missed the fact that kids weren't the only ones who needed that kind of support. That is until I became a parent too. In a world where people move frequently, it's often hard to know where to find good help. Add in a church culture that sometimes lacks authenticity—with people showing up looking as if they have it all together—and no wonder it's a challenge for parents to reach out for help. For those of us in ministry, you can add on top of that the unspoken expectation that, somehow, being in ministry automatically qualifies us to be great parents. (If only that were true…but it's not.) There have been times Lisa and I have felt isolated and alone in our parenting journey because we didn't feel we could admit our failings to anyone else.

Even though many assume I am an "expert" in parenting, I make mistakes and often feel woefully inept. It happens to the best of us, I guess. In my early days of parenting, after yet another parenting fail, I began to ask what would happen if parents were better supported in raising their kids in the faith. I wondered how kids would be affected if that were to happen. And that started me down a path of thinking about who I needed to be connected with to gain valuable support, encouragement, and practical wisdom. From there, I started to consider how I could facilitate creating a team of support for parents who often feel alone in their challenges.

PARENTS NEED TO KNOW THEY'RE NOT ALONE

When Gavin and Wendy*[1] had their first child, they were full of joy and love for the little blessing that had been given to them. Like so many young couples, they also quickly realized their schedule was no longer their own. That became an even stronger reality by the time they'd had their third child. But they would always maintain, "We wouldn't change this for the world!" With big church smiles planted on their faces, they'd rush their kids through check-in and make it into the service just as the music was ending.

While Gavin and Wendy felt blessed by their kids and their life as parents, it wasn't long until the cracks began to show. The realities of their new schedule meant that small group, quality friendships, and margin in their lives had taken a back seat for many years. One evening, after a run of sleepless nights and the usual parenting challenges, Wendy asked Gavin,

> How do we know if we're getting it right? Everyone else seems to have it all together with their kids. I have a teenager who doesn't talk to me anymore, a preteen who's overly emotional, and a toddler who's defiant every day. I love my kids, but how do I know if I'm getting it right?

Having three kids of my own, I can relate to Gavin and Wendy in so many ways. Having kids is a huge blessing and privilege. But there are seasons I feel tired and overwhelmed. It's during these times that Lisa and I need to know we're not alone and that we can count on good advice and support from others. Sadly, many parents don't have that kind of support.

Help Parents Develop a Team of Support

All parents need a team of support to help them on their parenting journey. It's important for them to be surrounded by people who can help and encourage them as they raise their kids. As with so many things in life, there's no manual with all the answers for questions parents will ask. But God often provides other people who can act as resources for those who need help. So even if you're not a parent yourself, it's imperative that you understand your role in connecting parents with a network they can rely on as they invest in their kids.

Let's take a look at some ways you and I can help parents develop that kind of network.

Practice radical hospitality. The first step in building a team of support for parents is to create a culture where parents can feel free to show up as they are. In *Why Nobody Wants to Go to Church Anymore*, Thom & Joani Schultz talk about the importance of practicing radical hospitality, which includes authentically welcoming people and accepting them no matter what.[2] Most parents carry a degree of insecurity about their parenting. And sadly, many have felt judged by the church in the past. Though I've often practiced radical hospitality with the kids and students in my ministry, I know there are also many times I haven't practiced it well with parents. We need to ensure that every parent in our ministry receives the message: "come as you are." They need to know they're not being judged and that there are others who understand what it's like to be imperfect at parenting. We need to go the extra mile to help parents feel welcome and accepted.

Connect parents with other parents. As I've mentioned in previous chapters, it's essential to connect parents with other parents in your ministry. Many parents feel as though they're the only ones who make mistakes or have kids with problems. But the truth is once parents sit down and begin to share stories with each other, it doesn't take long for them to realize that they aren't really any different from everyone else. Part of our responsibility is to connect parents with each other so they can find that kind of support in a community of faith.

Recruit seasoned parents. Parents with kids still at home need to know they're not alone and that there are others who've successfully gone before them. Some of the best partners you can have for your ministry are empty nesters who've "been there, done that, and got the t-shirt." Recently, I had one couple approach me about helping out in just this way. They told me,

> When we were parents, we often wondered if we were getting it right. Fortunately, we had a lot of support from some great people who were a few years ahead of us. Now we want to do the same for other parents. How can we help?

I don't get these kind of parents coming to me every day. But getting experienced parents involved doesn't usually take much. I've never had a parent whose kids are grown tell me "no" when asked to come alongside a younger parent. Those who've navigated through the parenting journey know just how important it is to have support along the way. There are plenty of experienced parents in your church who can make an eternal difference in the lives of the parents and kids currently in your ministry. Once you've recruited one, he or she can help you recruit others.

Promote small groups. Practically speaking, one of the best things we can do for parents is encourage them to be part of a small group or Bible study—especially if it means they'll be able to gather with other parents. We need to be huge cheerleaders of these types of ministries. When parents become invested in a small group or Bible study, they'll not only begin to experience authentic community, they'll also deepen in their faith. When that happens, there'll be a positive effect on how they function in their roles as parents.

Strengthen the connection between parents and volunteers. Effective children's and youth ministry volunteers not only invest in kids' lives, they understand and respond to the needs of parents too. In my ministry, there are several steps we take to help volunteers reach out to parents and also make it easy for parents to get in contact with the volunteers who are investing in their children. For example, all our small group leaders are provided with a profile card they can give to parents containing the leaders' pictures, a few sentences about themselves, and their contact information. Leaders are also trained and encouraged to make contact with parents at least once a semester (though some do it more). And every year we host a ministry open house that allows parents to experience the ministry environments their kids participate in and to meet with their kids' small group leaders.

In a previous church, Marve and Holly were two of my most faithful youth volunteers. They were empty nesters, had loads of time, and never seemed to run out of energy. The students loved them, and the parents did too. Given that their kids had all grown up and left the house, they had an amazing opportunity to encourage and support parents who were still trudging through the challenges of raising teenagers. Marve and Holly are not only great examples of how experienced parents can support parents who are still in the trenches, but also of the importance of connecting parents and volunteers as well. Parents grew to trust them and felt as though they were true partners with parents in raising their kids in the faith. Volunteers don't have to be experienced parents like Marve and Holly were, but they can still become a trusted source of encouragement and support to parents when the appropriate connections are made.

Many of the parents you and I minister to are working as hard as they can to give their kids the best things they can. But they're also feeling as though they're going it alone, struggling to know the best way to help their kids. God didn't make any of us to operate in isolation. He designed us for community and to be a support to one another. That's true for you and me, and it's true for the parents in our churches and communities. The challenge is for us to see ourselves as networkers—connecting parents to those who can give them the vital support and encouragement they need as they navigate through the parenting years.

GAME SUMMARY

Partnering with parents includes helping them connect with others in your church who can offer them encouragement and support.

PRACTICE DRILLS

1. Make a list of the opportunities your church or ministry offers to help parents connect with other parents. If your church doesn't currently offer any, brainstorm some things you could do to enable parents to interact with each other (don't forget to include opportunities that could piggyback on activities and events that are planned for their kids). Choose one idea, and begin planning it.

2. On a scale of 1 to 5 (with 1 being "come in if you must," and 5 being "we're excited you're here"), grade your ministry on how well you practice radical hospitality (authentically welcoming parents and accepting them no matter what). What grade do you think the parents you minister to would give you? What are some steps your ministry could take to improve in this area?

3. Create a list of parents in your church who have a reputation of being God-honoring and whose children are grown. Contact them and ask if they'd be available to come alongside parents whose kids are still at home to offer them encouragement and support.

4. Hold an open house for your ministry that enables parents to see the environments their kids participate in and to meet their kids' volunteer leaders. Provide your volunteers information cards they can give to parents that include the volunteers' pictures, a few sentences about themselves, and their contact information.

Endnotes

1 *Names have been changed.

2 Thom & Joani Schultz, *Why Nobody Wants to go to Church Anymore: And How 4 Acts of Love Will Make Your Church Irresistible*, (Loveland: Group, 2013), 76-78.

BIBLIOGRAPHY

Ackland, Donald F. "Deuteronomy." In *The Teacher's Bible Commentary*. Eds. H. Franklin Paschall and Herschel H. Hobbs. Nashville: Broadman and Holman Publishers. 1972.

Cabal, Ted, Chad Owen Brand, E. Ray Clendenen, et al., *The Apologetics Study Bible: Real Questions, Straight Answers, Stronger Faith*. Nashville: Holman Bible Publishers. 2007.

Children in Single Parent Families in The United States. https://datacenter.kidscount.org/data/tables/106-children-in-single-parent-families. Accessed August 10, 2020.

Comer, John Mark. *The Ruthless Elimination of Hurry*. Colorado Springs: WaterBrook, 2019.

Coxwain (Rowing). http://www.usrowing.org/Libraries/Coaching/Common_Rowing_Vocabulary.sflb.ashx. Accessed April 17, 2015.

Fields, Doug. *Purpose-Driven Youth Ministry: 9 Essential Foundations for Healthy Growth*. Grand Rapids: Zondervan Publishing House. 1998.

Freudenburg, Ben, with Rick Lawrence. *The Family Friendly Church*. Loveland: Group Publishing, Inc. 1998.

Harris, Jennifer L. Ph.D. *Kids Under the Influence: The psychology of marketing to young consumers*. http://www.psychologytoday.com/blog/kids-under-the-influence/201402/what-s-parent-do. Accessed December 5, 2014.

Haynes, Brian. *Shift—What it Takes to Finally Reach Families Today*. Loveland: Group Publishing. 2009.

Heath, Chip, and Dan Heath. *The Power of Moments: Why Certain Experiences Have Extraordinary Impact*. New York: Simon & Schuster. 2017.

https://www.barna.com/research/children-faith-formation/March 19, 2019.

http://www.bbc.com/news/magazine-24173194.

https://homeword.com/seminars/generation-2-generation/.

https://www.pewresearch.org/fact-tank/2020/02/05/how-americans-feel-about-the-satisfactions-and-stresses-of-modern-life/.

https://www.pewresearch.org/internet/2018/05/31/teens-social-media-technology-2018/. Accessed August 14, 2020.

https://www.theboatrace.org/the-basics.

https://www.visitlondon.com/things-to-do/event/8716237-boat-race.

Kimmel, Dr. Tim. *Connecting Church and Home*. Nashville: Randall House Publications. 2013.

Lawrence, Rick. *Jesus Centered Youth Ministry*. Loveland: Group Publishing, Inc. 2014.

Lewis, C.S. *The Problem of Pain*. San Francisco: HarperOne. 2015.

McGarry, Michael. *A Biblical Theology of Youth Ministry*. Nashville: Randall House Publications, 2019.

Nahai, Natalie. *5 Things You Need To Know About Marketing to Generation Y*. http://www.psychologytoday.com/blog/webs-influence/201305/5-things-you-need-know-about-marketing-gen-y. Accessed December 5, 2014.

Schultz, Thom & Joani. *Why Nobody Wants to go to Church Anymore: And How 4 Acts of Love Will Make Your Church Irresistible*. Loveland: Group. 2013.

Straw, Julie, Mark Scullard, Susie Kukkonen, and Barry Davis. *The Work of Leaders: How Vision, Alignment, and Execution Will Change the Way You Lead*. San Francisco: Wiley Publishers, 2013.

EPILOGUE

WHAT'S AT STAKE?

"After that generation died, another generation grew up who did not acknowledge the Lord or remember the mighty things he had done for Israel" (Judges 2:10). That verse has often made me pause and reflect on the importance of what I do. A whole generation had followed Joshua, and yet the generation that came after them was completely lost. Somewhere along the way that first generation failed to pass down their faith to their children. It's as though they'd forgotten the words Moses had spoken in Deuteronomy 6:4-9.

Depending on what study you read, it appears that droves of kids today are walking away from their faith despite having been involved in the church for most of their lives. Even though they've walked through the doors of children's and student ministries week after week, many of them are still deciding to exit their faith journey at graduation. The kids in our ministries will one day grow up to graduate from high school and head off to work or college whether they've developed a solid faith foundation or not. And while our ministries certainly have something to do with whether that faith foundation is developed, we have to embrace the reality that what we do is only a part of God's blueprint for passing the faith on to kids. If we want to see children and students develop the best faith foundation they can, we have to partner with parents and help them become the primary spiritual influencers in their kids' lives.

Even though I'm a pastor with a vision for kids, I can't lose sight of an even greater vision God has given me as a parent. I'm called to invest in the faith journeys of my three kids, helping them to place their trust firmly in Jesus and learn to live daily for him. At the time of writing, I have three kids who are aged three years apart and are currently elementary, middle school, and high school ages. We had nearly a decade in diapers and we have about a decade of paying for college to look forward to. I am not sure which is worse! Diapers or debt? (Sounds like a great student ministry game by the way). Even though we have some expensive college years ahead of us, I am extremely thankful to have been on an incredible faith journey with each of them. It's been fascinating to watch how God has shaped them as they grew, and so amazing to see how their personalities have intersected faith. Probably the greatest highlights so far have been seeing my two girls come to faith, baptizing them, and having led my youngest boy to accept Jesus as his Lord and Savior.

When our eldest, Emma, was baptized, we gathered at church with family and friends (her team of support) to celebrate a momentous milestone. As her proud dad and pastor, I was privileged to be the one to baptize her. As we waited for the service to begin, Emma and I had a precious moment together in a quiet room where we were able to talk and pray. As I looked at Emma, I was taken back to the delivery room in the hospital where we met for the first time. That day she came out screaming, eyes wide open, and incredibly alert. (Nothing like the teenager I see first thing in the morning these days.) After the doctors and nurses had taken care of her, and Lisa had held her for a while, I was able to hold her. She was a beautiful bundle of joy staring at me. My heart was captured in a moment! I remembered thinking, "There is nothing I would not do for you little girl. You mean the world to me." As I stood there as a first-time parent, tears formed in my eyes as I looked lovingly at this child who was absolutely dependent on us. I began to glimpse what the next few years would look like and consider some of the milestones she would pass. Eating, potty-training, walking, talking, reading, drawing, and writing. And then one day, accepting Jesus as her Lord and Savior…

Fast forward nearly a decade to her baptism and, once again, there I was eye to eye with Emma as we stood waiting for the service to begin. As I looked at my nervous little girl, I again began to glimpse the next few years together and consider some of her milestones ahead, but there was a big difference looming. At some point, this beautiful little girl wouldn't be dependent on us in the same way as she been up until that moment. In fact, at some point she would be growing into an independent, autonomous young adult. Over time our influence and investment would change as she would take greater ownership of her own faith journey. If, I am honest, I felt a little helpless, and in that moment, I felt more dependent on God than I had done in long time. Now I was feeling nervous! It was time for Emma to be baptized.

As a part of that service, I was able to hear her testimony of God's work in her life. The baby girl I once held in my arms was now sharing about her love for God and was verbalizing her dreams for the future. I kept asking myself how she got to be so big and where the time went. "Didn't she just learn to read? How did she learn so much in a short time?" I remember the exuberance and passion on her face as she articulated her faith and talked about her excitement to share that faith with her family and friends. I also remember feeling both fear and excitement when she said she was wondering if God might be calling her to be a missionary. That day, as I listened to my daughter, I wondered how God could have possibly used me—a broken vessel—as an instrument to pass the faith on to this maturing young girl. Regardless of my flaws and insecurities, God has blessed me to play a crucial role in her faith journey, and I'm forever thankful for that. It's a gift to have been on such an incredible journey with Emma so far! I've been able to see what it is like to live out Deuteronomy 6:4-9 not only in the ministries God has called me to lead, but I have also seen the vision become a reality in my own family. It's also a vision I want every parent to see come to life as God empowers them for an incredible faith journey with their kids. While I love the idea of being a hero to the kids in the ministries I lead, there is an even greater vision to make every parent in my influence to become the spiritual heroes in their kids' lives. Imagine what the faith of a generation would look like if you and I (and countless others) could make that vision become a reality?

God can and does use us to reach the next generation for Christ with the great programs and events we offer. What you and I do does make a difference. But as we discussed in the beginning of this book, our time with kids and students is limited compared to the time parents have with their kids. Parents have also been given a unique role that no one else can fill. Consequently, it's essential that we see the big picture of equipping parents to be the primary ones shaping their children's faith. It's not that we have to stop providing incredible programs and environments. It's more that we need to weave partnering with parents into the fabric of what we do. For decades we've been painting incomplete pictures by only focusing our attention on kids. It's time to complete those pictures and increase the effect of our ministries by taking greater steps to equip parents to reach the next generation for Christ.

Fast-forward ten or fifteen years from now. Think about a couple of the children or students in your ministry. Consider what their faith and lives would look like if their parents were better equipped to invest in their faith journeys. Imagine sitting down with their parents to hear all that God has done and is doing in their children's lives. Envision the tears of joy and excitement as they thank you for your support and constant encouragement. Can you see it? That's the better future you can look forward to as you partner with parents.

We need to reach and equip the next generation for Christ. Deuteronomy 6:4-9 gives us a blueprint for making that happen. Judges 2:10 shows us what's at stake if we don't. And being effective at it takes you, me, and the rest of the faith community committing to partner with parents as they pass their faith on to their kids.

Let the journey begin today. It's time to join parents on *their* journey!

The D6 Family App

Available in App Stores

Updated weekly, this app delivers resources designed to equip you for generational discipleship.

D6 Deuteronomy 6

What is **D6** ?

BASED ON DEUTERONOMY 6:4-7

A **conference** for your entire **team**

A **curriculum** for every age at **church**

An **experience** for every person in your **home**

Connecting
CHURCH & HOME
These must work together!

D6 CONFERENCE
ONCE A YEAR

DEFiNE & REFiNE Your Discipleship Plan

www.d6family.com

ONE HOUR
A WEEK

POWER OF
PARENTAL INFLUENCE

D6 EveryDay™

NOT JUST SUNDAY. EVERY DAY.

D6 EveryDay Curriculum . . .
cultivates generational disciple makers to live out what they learn.

- Continues the hallmark emphasis of generational discipleship
- Promotes biblical worldview development
- Emphasizes biblical literacy
- Addresses apologetics naturally throughout scope and sequence

- Tells the story of the Bible
- Emphasizes daily discipleship— not just Sunday discipleship
- Introduces enhanced discipleship tools for church and home
- Easily expands to facilitate a mid-week session

D6EveryDay.com
powered by D6Family.com